Being
Present

"Darren and I sat in meditation for a week, and I could clearly sense his ability to sink into stillness and be Present.... He has a beautiful way of writing and presenting spiritual teachings.... The feeling of Presence that Darren's book evokes gradually becomes an inner experience that you can keep tapping into, an experience that can go beyond reading his book."

— ESTHER EKHART, yoga and meditation teacher
and founder of the online yoga studio EkhartYoga.com

"*Being Present* provides insight into the nature of addiction, how it manifests and how it can be released. This clear and concise book is a useful tool for anyone who wants to understand addiction and recovery. In my work and in my personal recovery from addiction I can affirm that every addict needs to look beyond the substance or behaviours and into himself or herself as a person for the underlying cause. This always involves knowledge of thought patterns and emotions, and for many no sustained recovery would be possible without a spiritual program.

Ego is at the root of addiction, and learning new ways of letting go of unhelpful behaviours is a powerful growth in true self-awareness. The knowledge that I don't have to be trapped in my ego but can connect to a higher power comes as a tremendous relief and release for many addicts. To then develop a relationship with this higher self, experience the pleasure of connection and guidance, and enjoy the pathways of this journey brings deep healing for those used to unskilful means for dealing with pain.

This book from an experienced spiritual practitioner guides us carefully through to understanding what it means to be present and includes advice on how to seek help and support for those experiencing significant addictions. Presence is a powerful antidote to being lost in thought and craving, and I am happy to recommend this book̶͟͞ ͟͞ ̶͟͞ ̶͟͞ ̶͟͞ lerstanding of recovery."

suse worker

"Reading Darren's book *Being Present* feels like a meditation. In clear, simple language Darren describes the process of letting go of identification with our thoughts and feelings and invites us to a place of peace with what is. I have spent enough time with Darren to realize that this book is a transmission of his own deep practice of Presence. His teachings spring from his lived experience, and the authenticity of his words radiate from the page.

At this time humanity is in dire need of spiritual awakening, and this book is an invaluable guide to anyone interested in learning how to awaken in a way that is gentle and loving."

— JENNIE HASTINGS (SRI DEVI), yoga teacher and programmer
at Sivananda Ashram Yoga Retreat, Bahamas, and founder
of www.jenniehastingsyoga.com

"I met Darren in India at a yoga center several years ago, and I was struck by his Presence and kindness toward others. We later came to know each other, and I learned there were profound wisdom and spiritual teachings behind his outlook on life. Reading *Being Present* helps in keeping these teachings alive in daily life. For me practicing awareness through meditation and contemplating how to simplify my life makes me more peaceful and grounded in my often stressful working days.

As a medical doctor I strongly believe in having a holistic view of well-being, with physical and mental health being equally important. This book provides concrete guidance through different aspects of how you can improve your life when it comes to, for example, dealing with work-life balance, finding stillness, and overall cultivating Presence."

— JOHANNA ANDERSSON, medical doctor

Being Present

Cultivate a Peaceful Mind
through Spiritual Practice

Darren Cockburn

FINDHORN PRESS

Findhorn Press
One Park Street
Rochester, Vermont 05767
www.findhornpress.com

Text stock is SFI certified

Disclaimer
The information in this book is given in good faith and is neither intended to diagnose any physical or mental condition nor to serve as a substitute for informed medical advice or care. Please contact your health professional for medical advice and treatment. Neither author nor publisher can be held liable by any person for any loss or damage whatsoever which may arise from the use of this book or any of the information therein.

A CIP record for this title is available from the Library of Congress

ISBN 978-1-84409-746-3 (print)
ISBN 978-1-84409-760-9 (e-book)

Printed and bound in the United States by Lake Book Manufacturing Inc.
The text stock is SFI certified. The Sustainable Forestry Initiative® program promotes sustainable forest management.

10 9 8 7 6 5 4 3 2 1

Edited by Nicky Leach
Text design, layout and illustrations by Damian Keenan
This book was typeset in Adobe Garamond Pro and Calluna Sans Std with Bernhard Modern Std used as a display typeface.

To send correspondence to the author of this book, mail a first-class letter to the author c/o Inner Traditions • Bear & Company, One Park Street, Rochester, VT 05767, and we will forward the communication, or contact the author directly at **www.darrencockburn.com**

Contents

Foreword

Living in the present moment will enhance your relationships, help you experience joy, happiness and a lasting connection to a higher source that you cannot achieve any other way. In a world filled with many surface pleasures, it is easy to miss the most important connection; the connection to one's self.

Being Present is a roadmap that will take you on a journey to finding your own connection. Lessening the noise of the outside world that leads to unhappiness, addictions, unrest in the mind, anxiety, fear, destructive habits and patterns, *Being Present* will help you tap deep into your soul and unlock the connection that is your human right.

Darren Cockburn is a spiritual teacher by nature. His skilful articulation of complex spiritual concepts helps novice to advanced spiritual seekers alike cultivate a peaceful mind and spiritual connection. I had the pleasure of meeting Darren years ago on spiritual retreat and now consider him a close friend, confidant and teacher. Immediately taking to his warmth and loving nature, I found myself captivated by his presence. We talked for hours about life, love, mindfulness, meditation and spirituality. It quickly became obvious that Darren has been a long-time practitioner and has studied a wide range of religions, philosophies and spirituality.

When Darren told me he was writing a book, I was thrilled to know his knowledge would be transferred to the masses. Darren has a message that will resonate with all people from all walks of life. His experience, passion and understanding will help you find your own internal peace and ultimately transform your life.

As a wellbeing expert, I am exposed to many teachings, writings and practices. My book, *Back to Balance*, was written as a manual to help readers integrate mind, body and spirit to achieve ultimate health. I am constantly searching for and learning new ways to incorporate spirituality into my busy and sometimes stressful life. The key is to stay balanced and like everyone else, I am always looking for ways to keep myself centered. Darren provides structured teachings, reflections and exercises that have helped me stay present and cultivate a still mind.

If you are looking for spiritual practices to help you in everyday life, easily implementable solutions to cultivate a peaceful mind and spiritual connection, *Being Present* is the book for you. Through this easy to read manual, you will move deeper into your practice, gaining freedom from destructive patterns, thoughts and emotions. You will learn how to apply traditional spiritual teachings in your life. We are all faced with a wide range of stressors from our careers, relationships, addictions, financial pressures, illnesses, and responsibilities of all kinds. Learning how to manage these stressors is essential to living a balanced life. *Being Present* provides the tools to do so.

I wish you peace and love as you begin this very important journey to *Being Present*.

Cassie Sobelton

#1 Best-selling Author, Speaker and Wellbeing Expert
*Back to Balance: Crack Your Mind, Body, Spirit Code
to Transform Your Health*

www.CassieSobelton.com
Detroit, Michigan, United States

Chapter One

Introduction

A good place to start is to ask the question "What is Presence?" Keep that question in mind, as you are about to read a book which will point you towards the answer. Only you can make the connection, as the answer can be known, but not explained. You can ask me how it feels to bathe in the sea, and I can describe the temperature of the water, the sensation of the waves crashing against my body and the beauty found within the reflections from the sun. You can only know how this feels if you wade in and experience it for yourself. Even then our experience will be different every time because both the sea and us are constantly changing.

Being Present means connecting to something formless and unchangeable. However, the way we become Present is changeable, leading to a unique journey every time. The word "form" is used throughout this book. It includes everything within the universe, including thoughts, feelings, bodily sensations and anything that can enter the senses. Form represents everything that we can describe, down to individual particles within atoms. Formlessness or emptiness, on the other hand, is what cannot be described, only known or pointed towards.

You may have already discovered Presence. If you have, wonderful! You can use this book to deepen and increase the frequency of your experience. If not, reading this book may help you discover it. Experiencing even a brief flash of Presence is enough to allow you to reconnect with it again and again.

Characteristics of Presence

I will explain what Presence means to me in the form of six characteristics. This personal account is provided in the hope that my words point you in the right direction and may help you recall times when you have felt it for yourself. Your experiences of Presence, which may be described differently, connect to the same source. It is absolutely fine if you do not resonate with or understand the characteristics at this stage. Allow them to wash over you. They will become clearer as the book progresses.

The first characteristic is a still and quiet mind with no discursive thought. Discursive thought is the kind of thought that rambles around our minds in an uncontrolled way, without us being aware of it. When we are Present, we may be aware of odd thoughts coming to mind, which soon pass. The same is true of feelings such as excitement, anxiety, envy, happiness, sadness and so on. Occasionally a feeling will present itself and then pass. For example, we may experience a feeling of happiness. We can be directly aware of the components that make up the feeling of happiness, which may be certain bodily sensations and a smile, but there will be no discursive thought to accompany it. If we were lost in thought rather than being Present, we may be asking questions such as, "Why am I happy?", "How do I remain happy?" or "What will those people over there think about me being happy?" With Presence, we are simply aware and accepting of our direct experience with no discursive thought or questioning.

Freedom from discursive thought creates freedom from suffering. Suffering is different to physical pain. Physical pain is associated with the body and suffering is associated with our thoughts. The two are often connected. Physical pain can trigger suffering and suffering can trigger physical pain. Presence creates freedom from suffering and the opposite of suffering is peace. Suffering is created through craving. This is one of the central teachings of Buddhism. Whenever we get lost in discursive thought, there will always be craving towards pleasure or away from pain. These cravings operate using the realm of time and not the present moment, which is timeless. When we crave, our minds resist how things are in the present. Things are a certain way, which we cannot change now because they are, but we want them to be different. They cannot be different at this point in time. Thinking we can make them different now through thought and creating some fantasy in our minds is delusional and unhelpful. Presence on the other hand, which means being aligned with the present moment, accepts everything as it is at this point in time. This aligns us to how things really are and allows us to be peaceful and content. Once we understand these truths, the goal is to train the mind so that we can stay Present where thinking only occurs when we consciously enable it for practical purposes.

The second characteristic is connectivity to a transcendental source, allowing us to access peace, love and wisdom. This is a profound and powerful experience in which we feel greater than our egoic self. I am referring to the mind-made self or ego. This is the self that is lost in thought. This self temporarily disappears and is transcended by something much greater to which we feel simultaneously connected and a part of. An intrinsic part of this transcendental experience is receiving love and providing love. Regardless of where we are, what we are doing and whom we are with, we feel loved and held by something that we cannot experience with the usual senses. This is then reciprocated with an unconditional love for everything and everybody. It is a gentle and beautiful experience.

I use the word "love" throughout this book. Unless stated otherwise, love is the form that is expressed without wanting or conditions attached to it. It is not a romantic or conditional love, as conditional love is needy and always wants something in return for giving. The love referenced throughout this book is unconditional love or pure love. You may also hear this referred to by Buddhists as Metta or Loving Kindness. This beautiful and boundless love can be felt inside and outside of us when we are Present.

The third characteristic is a wise and loving creativity that can manifest in any form. For example, we might connect with a friend, perform an act of generosity or decide to stop doing something harmful. We may also create something physical that others can enjoy and make use of. It may not result in any speech or action and could simply present itself in the form of wise thoughts that serve some purpose in the future.

The fourth characteristic is a loving appreciation of beauty, which may be found in anything, including people, animals and objects. This is accompanied by a sense of oneness and connectedness. When we are Present, our sense of self is transcended, as is all separateness from form. The subject and object relationship we often experience with things is removed. It is no longer ourself and the rest of the universe, but the universe as a whole with a tiny fragment of that universe coming together for a moment, creating an illusion for others that there is something fixed about us. With Presence, we become awake and enjoy a much richer experience.

The fifth characteristic is skilfulness. My definition of skilfulness is, "The action that manifests from a state of Presence, including thought, speech, physical acts or stillness" Skilful action aligns us to give the universe what it needs for the totality to become more conscious. Another way of framing this is that we are wise enough to act from a place of love in the spiritual interest of ourself and others. It is impossible to determine through thought what skilful action is as our minds would need to understand the totality of the universe and the infinite stream of effects that our actions create. The human mind is sophisticated, but not that sophisticated. This is why skilful action can only originate out of Presence.

There are useful religious lists we can refer to, including Buddhist precepts and Christian commandments, pointing us broadly towards what is skilful. Occasionally these lists lead to opinions and distortion to suit personal or religious agendas. True skilfulness is like Presence in that it can be known, but never defined adequately by some list or manual. So our only option, if we want to be consistently and wholly skilful, is to surrender and allow the whole and complete intelligence to lead the way.

The sixth characteristic is fearlessness. Through Presence, we accept and reside within the present moment, which transcends the realm of time. We can consider the past or future without becoming lost in thoughts or emotions about them. Fear is always associated with the future, which can be anything from the next second to several decades away. Fear is also always associated with the past, which is where our conditioning creates its triggers. The ability to transcend time means we can transcend fear and there is nothing to be afraid of, including our own death. When we are Present, we know we can intrinsically accept what is, so there is never any resistance or fear about what might happen. Occasionally, we may experience physical feelings of fear within our body if there are immediate dangers whilst we are Present, which is natural and helpful. We can be aware of the fear whilst being simultaneously connected to a different realm that is fearless. The fearlessness holds the fear with love and allows it to pass.

A unique quality about Presence is its consistency and ultimately satisfying nature. In the world of form, things such as relationships, assets, our bodies and everything else will never ultimately satisfy us. They may satisfy us for a while, but then as circumstances change, which we can absolutely count on, the level of satisfaction will be eroded or lost altogether. Ironically, even when we think we are completely satisfied with something or someone, there is always background dissatisfaction there if we look closely enough, as we know deep within us that things do not ultimately satisfy us forever. Presence does not suffer from this inconsistency of satisfactoriness. It is always perfectly satisfying and the only thing that we can consistently depend upon. It achieves this because it is formless. Presence cannot be touched, heard, tasted, seen, inhaled or felt, making it very mysterious and unexplainable. We will realize when we become Present, as there is a very deep knowing that accompanies it. It cannot be fully explained, only known.

The Ego

The ego is referenced many times throughout this book and is covered in depth in Chapter Five. It is significant enough to justify a brief introduction here to set the scene for the subsequent chapters. The ego is the ultimate hindrance to being Present. Within this book, discussions on the ego are informed by the teachings of Eckhart Tolle [1]. My understanding is that Tolle describes the ego as thought and emotional patterns that are persistently repeated due to our strong identifications with them [2].

These thought patterns can be of a positive or negative nature. They can be about having something or not having something. Identifications include, but are not limited to, possessions, knowledge, roles, likes, dislikes, creations, opinions, resentments, appearances, beliefs, positive or negative comparisons, addictions, attachments from the past or fantasies about the future. The mind activities then give us a sense of who we perceive ourself to be, which is the delusion. To the ego, all identifications are viewed as beneficial. It believes that they are helping by adding to our false sense of self. The truth is quite the contrary because identifications reduce us rather than add to us.

Where there is suffering, there is the ego and its identifications. Once we are fully awakened and continuously Present, the ego is gone for good. All identifications are released, allowing us to respond creatively to every moment without any attachments or old patterns constraining us.

Presence & Mindfulness

Mindfulness is now popular through its widespread application outside of mainstream religion, including the areas of health and business. When I run mindfulness courses, I define mindfulness as, "Awareness and acceptance of bodily sensations, feelings and thoughts within the present moment". This book and other mindfulness teachings complement one another because they enable a connection with Presence. Nature, silence, quality spiritual teachings and a range of other sources, allowing us to gain perspective and transcend the thinking mind, are gateways into Presence.

As you read this book and develop your practice, keep in mind that mindfulness and Presence can coexist with thought. We are aiming to be the awareness that is observing the thoughts, not to control or stop them. A natural consequence of our spiritual practice is that our thoughts will become more skilful and reduce in volume over time, which means that we will enjoy a quieter and more peaceful mind. This process takes care of itself through surrendering to the present moment and does not require any intervention from our ego trying to control things.

Paradoxically, this gives us the perception that we are influencing or controlling our thoughts through our practice. This is not because we are consciously controlling, suppressing or guiding our thoughts. The truth is quite the opposite, in that we are relinquishing control and allowing our thoughts to be guided by an intelligence that transcends who we might think we are. With our practice, we actively refrain from trying to control our thoughts using thought. Controlling thoughts through thought is what causes our minds to become busy and confused. The reality is that things do not control themselves. We surrender to the present moment and allow that to guide us. Thinking then happens when required. Thoughts manifested through a state of Presence are creative, relevant, wise and loving. Speech and action follow thoughts naturally in the same manner because Presence uses thoughts as a vehicle to govern speech and action. The more we experience this, the more our faith in Presence develops and our practices flourish.

How to Cultivate Presence

We may experience glimpses of Presence and make a temporary connection to who we really are. The vision of our practice is to be continuously Present. There are many words and descriptions that point to this, including being "awakened", "enlightened" or "permanently at one with God". We let go of our egos completely, and what remains of our being is the consciousness out of which we arose. A few people may awaken suddenly through a significant experience after intense suffering or an instant spiritual realization. For most of us, our awakening is cultivated over time and follows a more gradual process. The same is true for the whole of humanity. As time progresses, we take more responsibility for our conditions and practice. Through doing this, we progress. The amount of time we are Present in any one instance is lengthened. The gaps between being Present and lost in thought are reduced and the depth of Presence we experience increases.

Being Present all the time and in every situation is unrealistic for most people, so it can be helpful to reflect on particular areas of our life and select one or two that we can focus on at any one point in time. As our Presence increases, it permeates into other areas without any conscious effort, so by working on one or two areas we are indirectly working on them all. Another option is to integrate Presence into a simple activity we do frequently, such as walking or eating. At the beginning of our practice, we can start with something relatively simple. Then, as our confidence grows, we can work on integrating Presence into more complex and challenging areas and activities.

Presence is cultivated through three approaches. The first is through structured practice. This covers activities practised on a regular basis, including meditation, yoga and studying spiritual teachings. Any activity that is being carried out with a primary objective of cultivating Presence falls into this category.

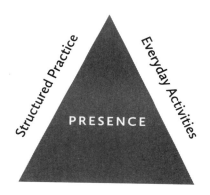

Three Approaches To Cultivate Presence

The second approach is through everyday activities where we are consciously striving to be Present. For example, we may be making a conscious effort to be more Present whilst walking, or brushing our teeth. The third approach is to change our conditions so that our life becomes more conducive to being Present. Examples here may include changing our job, letting go of certain relationships, working to release addictions, taking regular exercise, letting go of unhelpful habits and connecting with nature. As our Presence increases, so does our discernment and courage, enabling us to make bold decisions leading to more positive changes in our life.

Admiring the beauty of a landscape or gazing at the moon on a clear night can trigger a connection with Presence. It can feel as though these things we experience are providing the gift of Presence and creating a sense of inner peace or enjoyment. We should be grateful for such experiences. The beauty of the landscape or moon, in this case, is actually a gateway for accessing the Presence that is already there and available to us. Some experiences may have an opposite effect and lead to us becoming lost in thought. At a micro-level, this phenomenon applies to our internal experience, including bodily sensations, thoughts and feelings. Bringing to mind a picture of something beautiful may lead to Presence. Bringing to mind a difficult situation in the past that we are still resisting may lead us to become lost in thought. When we are challenged, there is always a choice to bring Presence into our experience, and the vision that underpins this book is to bring Presence into everything we do.

Over time and with practice we become more aware of when we are drifting off into discursive thought and we return to the present moment. This phenomenon can be likened to a spring. When the mind begins to wander without awareness, the spring is stretched and then uses its energy to snap back into its original shape as we transition back into Presence. In this analogy, the strength and resilience of the spring represent our capacity to be Present.

The Origins of Presence

From where does Presence originate? This cannot be explained and is impossible to pinpoint in the same way that we might pinpoint the source of water or light. Some religions use labels including the word 'God'. By itself, this is simply a three-letter word on a page or a sound that is made when verbalized. To help point us to the truth, people create commentary, imagery, organized religions and teachings. If these creations originate directly from Presence and retain their purity, they will lead people back into Presence.

Is the source within or outside of our bodies? When we open up our minds to Presence, it flows into us. Presence is its own source. We could claim that Presence is inbuilt and all we are doing is accessing something that is already there. Although this might be theoretically interesting, we do not need to understand where it comes from. We can enjoy Presence in the same way that we can enjoy gas, electricity or Wi-Fi within our homes without needing to understand the intricacies of how they are created or provisioned. When we switch on a device and send an email, there are many things taking place in our mind, through our fingers, technology and international data communications. Do we need to understand all that to send the email? No, we just press Send. We may need to understand part of the process if we have a design or maintenance job such as an engineer who works on data cables, or a mobile phone applications developer.

Some religious people and those with an active interest choose to intellectually explore the source. This is fine and can be an enjoyable pastime, as long as we do not *identify* with being able to fully understand it, otherwise the identification will stop us from making the connection. Also Presence cannot be understood through theoretical means. It is unnecessary for us to understand what we do not create or maintain in order to connect with it. We just need to know it's there. Presence does not need to be created or maintained. It is constantly accessible and maintains itself. Unlike services in the world of form, Presence has a perfectly consistent service level and all we really need to be concerned with is accessing it.

Presence & Religion

Different religions and philosophies use words and teachings that point to a spiritual goal such as enlightenment or becoming one with God. The ultimate goal, as I see it, is to be continuously Present. When I reflect on my practice, which is aligned with the pointers presented within this book, I can say categorically that my life has been transformed in terms of personal ethics, peace and happiness.

I was a practising Buddhist for a few years and have connected with other religions and movements lightly through reading, friends, spiritual retreats and travel. What I have learned through my own experience and discussion with others is that Presence and the teachings within this book may integrate with other spiritual and religious endeavours that are pointing to the same single truth.

Through Presence, it will become clear as to whether an existing spiritual or religious endeavour is appropriate for us. It is important that when we are involved in a religion, we retain our sense of self. This is not the ego-based mind-made self or another self that has been created for us by our religion, but our true self which is the real essence of us. We must never become lost in a religion or anything else for that matter. When we are lost in a religion, we are lost in thought and when we are lost in thought, we cause harm. Religions can be a great help to people who need their structures, teachings, network of friendships and other support on offer. In these instances, if we can retain our true sense of self, it may well be beneficial to integrate into a religion for a period of time and in some cases for the whole of our life.

How Our Thoughts Change

Presence enables freedom from thought. When we are Present, we have perspective on our own mind. We can choose to think or choose not to think, and never be lost in our thoughts. Over time, it becomes as easy to stop thinking and experience a quiet mind as it does to mute a mobile phone. Thinking is no different to any other tool in that it works well if it is used consciously for a job that needs doing and then placed down to rest. It does not make sense to carry physical tools around with us if they are not needed and the same applies to thinking. Thinking is analogous to a power tool in that if it is used constantly for a long period of time without a rest, the functioning and quality of service it provides degrades. Used without awareness, it can cause harm. Once our thinking has served a specific purpose, the mind can rest and we can let go of thought. A few people who have undergone very sudden spiritual transformations may instantly develop the skill of being able to let go of thought on demand, but for the majority the ability to actually decide when to think and when not to think evolves gradually over time.

The Prompts to Write This Book

One morning during my regular meditation, I received a calling to write a spiritual book. The thought popped into my head and was completely out of the blue. I disregarded it and later in the day I walked into town. I entered a shop that sold second-hand goods to raise money for a mental illness charity. I'd passed by the shop a few days before and experienced a pull to enter it, which I resisted at the time. On entering the shop, I was greeted by a friendly and curious elderly woman who was a customer there. I remember her being very alert and Present with sparkling bright blue eyes. She asked if she could read my palm. During the reading, she told me that I was able to teach and that I would write a book. It felt most peculiar that this should happen within a few hours of the calling during my meditation.

These two events happening together on the same day coupled with a strong intuition convinced me that this book needed to be written. So I got to work on it in my spare time, which was usually on an evening after I had finished work for the day. Within one year, the book was complete.

Prior to writing the book, I had been reading and listening to spiritual teachings extensively, including those of Eckhart Tolle. Tolle introduced me to 'Presence', which inspired the writing[1]. For years, I had binged on teachings, retreats and communication with those who I believed were more spiritually evolved. It felt like I had consumed so much and writing this book provided me with a way of digesting it all. Much of the content is based upon teachings I have extracted from other sources. The synthesis between these teachings, the structure of the book and my own insights are original and unique at the time of writing, to the best of my knowledge.

Using This Book

The book has been developed in such a way that each chapter provides a component in an overall framework or structure within which you can operate your spiritual practice. The chapter headings on the contents page show the wide variety of areas covered. The diversity of each chapter represents the magnitude of the opportunity to practise being Present. The fact that you can incorporate practice into everything you do means this wonderful gift has the potential to be realized in every area of your life and for the whole of your life. To start with, it is fine if you focus your practice on a few areas or even a single area. Those who like to make plans and create goals, can take a more structured approach. Whatever your personal style, once you are on the path, something accessible by you which transcends your thoughts will guide your practice.

The book can be read from cover to cover or as a reference guide. You may choose to read the whole book first and then return to chapters where you need to go deeper. The guidance in the chapters of this book has been introduced to inspire you in different ways at different times so reading the chapters multiple times may prove beneficial. You may find that you need to take a break after reading a relatively small amount of content. If you feel 'full' at points, it is best to stop for a while and continue again after you have digested what you have just read.

Throughout the book you may hear certain words repeated such as 'Presence' and 'ego' without understanding fully what they mean. This is absolutely fine. There is no need to get hung up on specifics and definitions. As you continue to read, reflect and read again, the meanings behind these words will become clearer.

Chapter Two covers the centricity of the body within spiritual practice, providing some practical guidance that demonstrates how caring for the body and giving it the attention it needs leads to better health and increased Presence. We can use our body as a tool to raise our level of consciousness. Areas covered include exercise, diet, breathing, tiredness, illness, pain and sexuality. Our interactions with people are considered in Chapter Three.

This is a highly influential area for us, deserving careful consideration. The guidance helps us understand the impact that different people have on our own personal state, along with providing a range of pointers on communication, friendship, how we handle difficult relationships, listening and solitude. The relevance of meditation is introduced in Chapter Four, with guidance on technique and integration into our day-to-day activities.

Chapter Five introduces the main internal hindrances that lead to us being lost in thought, including the role of the ego. Guidance on simplifying our lives and using simple situations and activities to become more Present is provided in Chapter Six. Chapter Seven helps us understand how addictive thought patterns and behaviours hinder us, pointing the way to action we can take to reduce them and ultimately let them go. The gifts of stillness, spaciousness and nature, which are all gateways into Presence, are introduced in Chapter Eight. Chapter Nine explores the core practice of acceptance and how it can be cultivated. Chapter Ten explains how we can hold the relative importance of what we do with lightness and ease through taking an absolute perspective on our life. The areas of work and other forms of service are discussed, giving us the opportunity to review our current work situation and take responsibility for initiating change if required. The final area of practice, examined in Chapter Eleven, is that of integrating spiritual teachers, religion and study. To conclude, Chapter Twelve provides guidance on how we can bring all these areas together and create a structure to support our ongoing practice.

At the end of each chapter, you will find sections labelled 'Points for Reflection', which repeat a short list of some of the key elements from the main text of the chapter. To support your learning, you are advised to reflect on each point in the context of your own personal situation and understanding. This should be undertaken slowly and mindfully, followed by a pause for reflection after each point. It may also help to reflect with friends or in a group. Refrain from using the points for reflection as an alternative to reading the main content of the chapters. The main content and key points must be used together to provide the context of the teachings and the greatest opportunity to reflect and learn. You may also return to the key points from each chapter as a reference point in the future.

After the points for reflection, learning activities are provided. These take the form of questions and opportunities for you to take action and make changes based on the content of the chapter. Review each of the learning activities and decide what you would like to take forward into your practice. It may be that you follow up on none, one or all the activities. Less is often more. Consider doing fewer activities over a given time period and doing them well. This will be more beneficial than starting a larger number of activities and failing to benefit from any of them. Go for quality rather than quantity. You have your whole life to work through these activities and can return to them at a later date if you wish.

This book will introduce you to spiritual concepts and practical interventions you can make in your life conditions and mindset to cultivate more Presence. Consider exposing yourself to other spiritual teachings in-between reads. All quality spiritual teachings point to the same source. I use the word *quality* to denote the fact that they have been created out of a state of Presence rather than from the ego. These teachings can help you discover Presence for the first time and also deepen your experience. In addition, the content found here will guide you towards sustaining Presence for longer periods of time.

Being Present has also been written to support your personal practice. By this, I mean that any pointers that you wish to apply should be applied to yourself as opposed to advising others. The content should not be read so that you can 'fix' a friend or family member. Through working on yourself, you will inspire and teach people naturally and spontaneously. The best thing that you can do for others is to become more Present yourself. Only through doing this can you increase your love for them. On a related point, the content of this book is written for adults. Being Present with children is encouraged and highly beneficial. Teaching them how to connect with Presence in the same way that you might teach an adult may cause problems as they have different development needs. Please consult more targeted teachings for parents if you have children and wish to support them in this area.

Finally, I would like to reference the two main sources of teachings that have inspired this book and my own insights. The first source is Eckhart Tolle's teachings and the second source is Buddhist teachings which are central to many of the approaches and concepts outlined. I hope that what you read will be instrumental in pointing you towards a way of life that is peaceful, happy and full of love.

POINTS FOR REFLECTION

- This book will point you towards Presence. Only you can make the connection and know it for yourself.

- Characteristics of Presence:
  - A still and quiet mind with no discursive thought.
  - Connectivity to something that transcends us. An intrinsic part of this transcendental experience is receiving love and giving love.
  - A wise and loving creativity that can manifest in any form.
  - A loving appreciation and experience of beauty.
  - Skilfulness, aligning us to give the universe what it needs for the totality to become more conscious.
  - Fearlessness.

- Suffering is different to physical pain and is created by our thoughts.

- Suffering is created through craving, which is one of the central teachings of Buddhism.

- Skilfulness is the action that manifests from a state of Presence, including thought, speech, physical acts or stillness.

- Our only option, if we want to be consistently and wholly skilful, is to surrender and allow the whole and complete intelligence to lead the way.

- Presence does not suffer from an inconsistency of satisfactoriness. It is always perfectly satisfying and the only thing that we can really count on in our life.

- Anything natural that allows us to gain perspective and transcend the thinking mind is a gateway into Presence.

- Our practice should be to aim for being continuously Present, also known as being awakened, enlightened or permanently at one with God.

- Presence can be cultivated using structured practice, everyday activities and changing the conditions of our life.

- The experience of external form can trigger a connection with Presence.

- Being lost in thought is the opposite of being Present.

- Religious organizations can be a great help to people who need and benefit from their structures, teachings, network of friendships and other support.

- The demands of an organized religion may lead to us becoming lost in that religion if it is out of alignment with our true purpose.

- Aim for regular practice and steady progress rather than speed and perfection.

- Presence enables freedom from thought. When we are Present, we have perspective on our own mind.

OPTIONAL LEARNING ACTIVITIES

- Recall occasions when you have experienced the six characteristics of Presence:
    - A still and quiet mind with no discursive thought.
    - Connectivity to something that transcends us.
    - A wise and loving creativity that can manifest in any form.
    - A loving appreciation and experience of beauty.
    - Skilfulness, aligning us to give the universe with what it needs for the totality to become more conscious.
    - Fearlessness.

- List some of your identifications. What does your ego identify with? Examples include possessions, knowledge, roles, likes, dislikes, creations, opinions, resentments, appearances, beliefs, positive or negative comparisons, addictions, attachments from the past or fantasies about the future.

- Bring awareness to when you are lost in thought in your daily activities and see if you can regain Presence by bringing your attention back to something real like the breath or the energy in the body.

Chapter Two

Body

The human body is a wonderful creation. It is our vehicle through life that enables such a rich experience including many pleasures. At the same time, it can indirectly trigger suffering if we allow ourself to react to its issues unskilfully[3] instead of responding wisely. This is the paradox of the body and the paradox we observe in many things that serve us within the realm of form. On the one hand, we can benefit and enjoy the pleasure. On the other hand, we are challenged and experience the pain. The realm of form gives with one hand and takes with the other. Presence transcends the body in the same way that it transcends our feelings and thoughts. When we are Present, we are free from mind-generated suffering. We can be at peace and love our body regardless of its condition whilst also taking responsibility for its needs.

When we are experiencing unhelpful thoughts about the past or future, it is wise to direct our awareness into the body and look for physical pain. I often catch myself thinking negatively and being lost in thought when I am unaware of pain. The pain may be anything from a subtle ache to something more severe. Bringing awareness to physical pain may not remove it, but it will remove the suffering. There is a difference between pain and suffering and an opportunity to reduce both. Pain is experienced physically within the body and suffering is experienced through thought. Some of the time, we can reduce pain in the body by taking action such as getting appropriate exercise or taking medication. The antidote to our mind-generated suffering is Presence. The mind does not cause any stress or suffering when we are Present. We can be aware and accepting of physical pain whilst simultaneously experiencing a peaceful mind.

Sometimes being lost in thought is triggered by uncomfortable bodily sensations, which are caused by emotions. For example, anxiety may manifest as a stomach ache or tension in the shoulders. Stress could manifest in the form of a headache. The body always reacts for a reason, which makes it a useful tool in diagnosing underlying issues. Body awareness is enabled by Presence and enables Presence. When you are aware of the body, you are Present and when you are Present, you have awareness of the body. Presence may not alleviate pain, but it will always remove suffering. Even great spiritual leaders such as Jesus and the Buddha experienced physical pain. It is part and parcel of being human.

Looking After Our Bodies

By following general advice on eating a balanced diet and taking regular exercise, we can benefit from a healthier body, which makes Presence easier to cultivate. You may recall a time in the past when you reacted unskilfully to a person or situation when you were ill or tired. At other times, when the body is well, life can feel much easier to navigate. Tuning into the body makes it possible to understand what it needs and to respond accordingly. What our body needs may be different to what our mind craves for. When we are craving something that depletes the body rather than nourishing it, the mind is attempting to escape from emotional pain using an addictive thought pattern. Addictions are explained further in Chapter Seven.

Allowing intoxicants to enter the body lowers our awareness and causes us to become lost in thought. To cultivate Presence, we can consider the option of working towards letting go of intoxicants altogether. For example, many people tell us that they can have a glass of wine or a beer without it adversely impacting their awareness. Some people believe their mind is functioning normally because they are not yet aware enough to understand the effects of the alcohol. An example of this is the drunk at a party who is telling everybody they are sober. I cannot comment for you, but I know that in my own case, even a single glass of wine or beer makes a difference to my awareness.

Never torment the body. For example, if we are hungry, we should eat and if we are tired, we should rest. There may be occasions where this is not possible, but generally speaking, and where practical, we should give the body what it needs when it needs it. Failure to meet the needs of the body over a sustained period of time leads to illness. We should honour the body and use our mind skilfully to serve it. One of the roles of the mind is to be a good servant to the body. The mind's ultimate role is to be a conduit for expressing love towards everything and everybody, including our own bodies.

Working with Tiredness & Illness

It is possible, albeit challenging for most, to be Present even when faced with difficult conditions such as tiredness and illness. We can experience physical pain, whilst being free from the unhelpful action and suffering that often follows, such as complaining, blaming and negative thoughts. Tiredness and illnesses are both great opportunities for practice. We can approach them from two angles. Firstly, by accepting our experience and secondly by taking action if it is possible to address the causes, thus helping us to stay well in the future.

For most, it is easier to stay Present by taking action to reduce the likelihood of getting ill or tired rather than being Present when faced with the conditions. To accept tiredness or illness, one must bring awareness to the associated bodily sensations, thoughts and feelings that constitute it. Tiredness and illness are both subjective feelings which have their constituent parts. Tiredness may be a combination of aching parts of the body, a foggy head, sore eyes or other bodily sensations. To stay Present, we must be constantly aware and vigilant of our bodies. Otherwise, emotions are triggered and before we know it we are lost in thought and the cycle of mind-generated suffering begins. Recurrent tiredness and illness are often caused through being in a consistent state of resistance to what is. In these cases, we are receiving feedback from the body that things need to change.

Tiredness is a manageable condition and can be experienced peacefully when it is accepted rather than resisted. We can bring acceptance to tiredness in two ways. The first is to sleep or take proper rest by letting go of doing anything physically and mentally. The second is to continue with our activities whilst at the same time being aware of how the tiredness is feeling within the body. If we are drinking a cup of tea and feeling tired, we can be aware of the taste of the tea and be simultaneously aware of the symptoms of tiredness within the body. On the flip side, there are ways in which we can resist tiredness. The first is to rest physically, but feel anxious and frustrated because we have an expectation that we should be busy doing something. The second way to resist tiredness is to go about our activities and ignore the experience of tiredness within the body. This could be through psychological repression or by physically masking it through the use of a stimulant such as caffeine. Resisting tiredness ultimately leads to further tiredness. So when we are tired, we must rest or continue our activities whilst simultaneously being aware of the experience of tiredness until it passes.

It took decades to appreciate that my body and consequently my thoughts reacted to processed sugar, alcohol and certain types of food, which triggered tiredness. Repressing the tiredness brought resistance and unpleasantness to my everyday activities which I would usually enjoy, such as working and being with my children. Rather than bringing awareness and acceptance to the bodily sensations, my mind would dodge them, creating a variety of stories about the past and future. This made me unhappy and impacted those I connected with at the time. During these times I was in a dream-like state. The unpleasant feelings and thoughts fuelled the tiredness to an even greater level. Often this downward spiral would temporarily burn me out and I would need to take lots of rest before resuming my everyday activities. By making some relatively small dietary changes, I found I could sustain good energy levels and it felt like a weight had been lifted from my shoulders. Everything became so much easier, lighter and enjoyable.

People often use stimulants such as caffeine or foods with a high sugar content as a reaction to tiredness. Stimulants in whatever shape or form push the body beyond its natural level of operation, creating physical and psychological stress. If stimulants are used consistently in this way, the risk of physical or mental illness is increased greatly. The ideal is to understand and respond to the body's needs with a natural diet. It can be a challenging transition and may mean learning about alternative foods and where to source them. In many countries, the popular, inexpensive food and drink on offer are full of stimulants and chemicals, making it challenging and expensive to acquire natural products. Whilst the world is waking up, we must be creative in sourcing our food and strive to look after our bodies. Where possible, we should give the body natural foods without intoxicating ourself and become more aware of times when we need to rest. Tuning into our body in this way enhances physical health and cultivates a peaceful mind.

If we have times when we are tired, but it is inappropriate to rest, we can intensify our awareness or increase our concentration on an activity to create energy. Concentration reduces the chance of us drifting off into thought. Intense awareness allows us to better monitor our thoughts, speech and action. Staying skilful is naturally more challenging when we are tired. I have noticed that my mind has some inappropriate strategies it deploys to help me stay active when I need to rest. One of them is creating mischievous and unskilful thoughts about people or situations. These thoughts are stimulating and I suspect it is the mind's way of trying to create energy to keep me alert. The more I am aware of this, the less frequent and intense it becomes. I notice the same thing when running workshops with groups of people. After a while they may become giddy, mischievous and disruptive, which signals to me it is time for a break. We must bring awareness to our unhelpful thought patterns during tiredness. Awareness enables acceptance, which enables letting go.

Having an illness is a special opportunity to practise acceptance as it brings us challenges to work with that are created by the ego. Our egos do not want us to be ill, as they feel threatened. They feel threatened that the illness may reduce us in some way, rendering us weak or even ending our life. The ego reacts using its favourite weapon: resistance. This shows itself in a number of ways, including denying the body rest and carrying on without the necessary adjustments to support recovery. Our egos may create stories about things going wrong if we are not involved in our usual activities we had planned or try and fool us by denying the illness exists, despite symptoms or a diagnosis. Unless we are fully accepting of our illness, the ego will be at work and whenever this happens, we have an opportunity to evolve through becoming aware of it.

We observe the ego at work by recognising when we are lost in thought. We become lost in thought during illness if we are denying pain or discomfort rather than accepting it. We also become lost in thought if we are denying our bodies what they need and pushing on with our daily activities without making adjustments such as taking extra rest, medication or advice we receive from healthcare professionals who usually have more knowledge about our condition than we do. This is due to a disconnection between the natural needs of the body, which are always real, and the deluded views that we create in our minds. Body awareness and learning from our own suffering help us to see clearly.

During times of illness, we manage our level of Presence using the same approaches that we use at any other time. We adjust our conditions to create a more conducive and kinder environment for ourself. We remember to practise using our breath and body awareness. Simplifying life during times of illness helps create more space where we can allow the mind and body to slow down and recover. If we fail to intervene, nature will intervene for us. Sometimes, the body will cease to function for a while, forcing the required rest, and the timescales for recovery may elongate. We should make an effort to practise being Present as much as we can when we are well and our physical conditions are good. By doing this, we are more likely to remain Present during the more challenging times. Present moment awareness enables us to connect with the space between the body and mind, which means that we can see their separateness clearly. When we see their separateness and the links between them, we can enjoy a peaceful mind amidst an uncomfortable or painful body. So by cultivating the ability to view body and mind as separate entities whilst acknowledging that they influence each other creates freedom.

Sometimes we have issues with the body that cannot be rectified. An example of this for me was developing tinnitus as a result of listening to loud music. My doctor told me there was little I could do to influence the condition and that it was incurable. So I bring full acceptance to it. This does not remove the tinnitus, but it does provide me with a sense of peace and freedom from any mind-generated suffering. When I am aware of the high-pitched noise that tinnitus creates in my head, I know that I have regained Presence.

We can consider Presence as an effective tool to support illness and guide us towards recovery. It helps with any physical complaint from a common cold to a life-threatening illness. It is also a highly effective pain-management system. Temporarily simplifying our life during illness through reducing or removing some daily activities is a golden opportunity to create spaciousness in which we can practise and stay Present.

Managing Pain through Presence

The difference between physical pain and suffering is important and worthy of repeating. 'Pain' relates to the body and 'suffering' relates to the mind. There is a link between the two. Pain can trigger suffering and suffering can trigger pain. Pain and suffering can also create a looping effect whereby pain causes suffering (or vice versa), which causes more pain, which causes more suffering and so on. Presence enables us to decouple pain, and suffering allowing us to be free from suffering whilst we are in pain.

I recall a time when I was on a flight with my daughter. The woman beside us was petrified when the plane ascended into the air. I spent a couple of minutes reassuring and comforting her. Later in the flight, she was explaining how she had been an insomniac for many years. The main factor preventing her from sleeping was her resistance to the condition. Being in resistance to an issue prevents you from seeing clearly and working through it effectively. She felt she should not be an insomniac; that it was bad and causing her constant frustration. The antidote here was acceptance. The woman with the sleep issue needed to bring awareness and acceptance to all the experiences that accompanied the condition, including her sensations of tiredness in her body, her feelings of frustration, and her unhelpful thoughts. Doing this would calm her mind, leaving her in a better position to make some helpful adjustments and improve her sleep.

The woman asked me how she could bring acceptance to the condition. I asked her if she had brought acceptance to any other difficult conditions or situations. She told me she had accepted that she could not go on holiday for decades due to her late husband's agoraphobia. She also told me that her feet were swollen and in pain from the flight. I asked whether she was frustrated about the pain in her feet and she replied, "No, I am not frustrated. I accept that this happens on a flight and do what I can to manage it." Clearly, she was at peace with having swollen feet. She had effectively managed to separate out the pain from the suffering. She was experiencing pain in her feet, which she could do nothing about at that point in time. Her mind was accepting the situation, allowing her to be peaceful. Later she asked me what she could do to resolve the sleep situation. I explained that it would help greatly to bring acceptance to insomnia in the same way that she had brought acceptance to her husband's agoraphobia and her painful feet. Acceptance is covered in more detail in Chapter Nine.

We can work with physical pain using two methods. Firstly, bringing awareness and acceptance to the pain, which means we stay Present. This leaves our mind peaceful and prevents it from generating suffering and creating further pain in the body. Secondly, we identify actions we can take to help relieve or remove our physical pain, such as taking medication, exploring alternative therapies or seeking medical advice. If there is nothing further we can do, then we continue to bring acceptance to the pain. There is a theme of awareness and acceptance running through the whole process, which creates a space between the pain and our thoughts. Physical pain may lead us into a state of Presence. Many people have experienced rapid spiritual progress through having to deal with severe illness and physical pain.

Whether we are experiencing pain, other bodily sensations, emotions or thoughts, we always have two choices. We either get lost in thought or we stay Present. Through cultivating the link from physical pain to Presence, we are training the neural pathways in our brains to do the same with other experiences. This is analogous to when we cultivate Presence in meditation through concentration on the breath or some other object. We are training ourself to come back to the present moment and this bears fruit inside and outside of meditation or pain management. Pain and suffering should never be consciously triggered. When they arise naturally, they can be viewed as an opportunity to practise.

I have experienced a painful muscular spasm on a regular basis for most of my life. I had the problem examined by a consultant. The first option was surgery with some unpleasant side effects and the second option was to accept the pain on the basis that it would have no other long-term detrimental effect on my health. I opted to accept the pain.

Over the years I have managed the pain using various techniques and medications. Learning about becoming Present and using that to gain freedom from the associated mental suffering has been liberating. It allows the pain to pass sooner as resistance does not fuel it. I recall a time when I was experiencing pain from this condition whilst dining in a restaurant. I had a good walk ahead of me back to the hotel where I was staying and made a conscious decision to fully accept the pain. I stayed Present, which allowed my mind to become peaceful. The pain became more intense as I returned to my hotel room and all I could manage to do at the time was to lie down on the bed. I entered a very sublime and blissful state. The pain was still there within my body, but I was intensely Present and free from any suffering associated with it. It was a liberating experience and to this day, the memory leaves me feeling very positive and empowered.

Whilst exercising or going about any of our daily activities, we can bring awareness to discomfort or pain we experience within the body. Discomfort during exercise helps build physical strength. Yoga operates in this way. Leg raises may create discomfort in the abdomen whilst at the same time strengthening it. Discomfort created through lifting weights will have the same effect.

Pain is different to discomfort, as it is harmful. I experience discomfort as a dull, moderately uncomfortable ache in one or more parts of my body whereas pain has a sharper texture and manifests suddenly. We should always take responsibility to change our conditions to reduce or remove physical pain where possible.

Exercise & Movement

Exercise and movement can be used as a channel to help us become Present as it supports awareness of the body. For example, when we are running, we may be aware of our body through faster breathing and sensations in the legs. If we are in a yoga pose, we will feel some discomfort as the body stretches, which is part of the strengthening process. For some, these bodily sensations are easier to be aware of than their more subtle counterparts we experience when we are still. Through being more aware of the body, the thoughts reduce and become less intrusive, which is why people often report a feeling of calmness after exercise.

When I find myself lost in thought during exercise, I will play with the intensification. Intensifying the exercise intensifies the sensations in the body and promotes direct body awareness. For example, if I am in a yoga pose and lost in thought, if it is safe to do so, I will stretch deeper. This allows me to experience more discomfort in the stretch, connect to the discomfort and then let go of the thought. If I am lost in thought whilst running, I will run a little faster, which produces a similar result as the sensations in the legs and intensity of breath increase. There needs to be intelligence within this method of increasing the intensity which protects the body from overworking and damage. The intelligence comes through the state of Presence. We can also be lost in thought if our exercise is too intensive. In these cases, lowering the intensity will help to regain Presence. The intention should be to establish a level of intensity that enables us to work to an intelligent and safe edge. This is good for the body and our spiritual practice.

We can bring awareness to our exercise and understand whether it is cultivating a calmer mind or causing the mind to become lost in thought. If we find ourself lost in thought whilst exercising, this means that we are resisting our experience and the thoughts are acting as an escape mechanism. We should either make a conscious effort to accept the exercise fully or change the exercise in some way through technique, intensity or duration.

The Breath

The breath is one of the most accessible tools we have at our disposal to help us stay Present. It is available to us from the initial breath we take as a newborn baby to the final breath we take prior to our death. It is regulated by the body's intelligence and can also be controlled through breathing techniques such as those found in yoga. In our practice we may simply observe its natural state. Whilst conscious control of the breath is not essential, it can help to take a few deeper conscious breaths from time to time. Controlling the breath temporarily by lengthening and deepening it can bring us into the present moment. You may have heard people say, "take a deep breath" during times when you are challenged. There is wisdom in this as it promotes awareness.

The breath is forever changing. Its length, texture, sound and depth are all subject to change. Like all form, the breath is not absolutely real, but we think it is real and call it 'the breath'. The breath has been used as a meditation object for thousands of years. It was central to the Buddha achieving enlightenment over two and a half thousand years ago and some scholars believe that people were meditating using the breath long before then. So the breath has a great lineage within spiritual practice. When we look closely, we see that we cannot find anything fixed about it. So it is an illusion, which makes it a great object to contemplate as it teaches about impermanence and insubstantiality – two of the central teachings of Buddhism. Impermanence is the truth about things constantly changing. This links to insubstantiality, which is the truth that everything we conceptualize is not fixed or real, because things are constantly in a state of flux. Even us humans are not absolutely real, despite us spending most of our life thinking we are!

When we have some or all our attention on the breath, we are Present. This is because the breath is not a subject of the past or future such as a thought fantasy. It is real and present now. The breath protects us from our minds creating unhelpful self-referential stories and other hindrances. So by connecting to the breath, we are connected to the present moment. Try accessing the breath now. Become aware of the breath whilst you read these words. It is possible to be aware of the breath and be aware of other things such as what we are reading, sounds, sights and things entering the senses. The beauty of the breath is that when we give it just a small amount of attention, one of two things happens. If we need to think, our thinking is skilful, relevant and creative. Alternatively, our thinking ceases altogether for a while, leaving the mind in a clear and peaceful state.

Becoming aware of the breath after being lost in thought for a period of time signals that we have returned to the present moment. We should always be grateful when we are aware of having been lost in thought. If we anchor a small amount of our attention to our breath, unconscious and habitual thinking ceases, leaving us Present and aware. Being lost in thought leads to unskilful thoughts and suffering. We sometimes become lost in thought when the mind tries to work out a solution to a problem it cannot solve, creating mental rambling and looping. These types of thought patterns are the result of our craving and the ego's need to control things. When we watch our experience closely, we realize that after we have been lost in thought, we experience a negative energy in the body and the scale of this depends on the grossness of the thoughts and any unskilful speech or action which follows. The more we are Present, the less we crave and the less we become lost in thought.

We can train ourself to anchor some awareness to the breath through meditation, which is discussed in Chapter Four. This is helpful for some people, but not for everybody. Another option is combining breath awareness with movement practices such as yoga or Tai Chi. There are endless opportunities to practise awareness of the breath in our day-to-day activities. To start with, it is easier to practise with simple activities such as sitting on a train, washing the dishes or brushing our teeth. Remember, that this practice does not require us to focus exclusively on the breath. Just a small amount of awareness is sufficient to remain Present.

We can incorporate mini breathing meditations into various points of the day in-between activities, at scheduled times or when we are waiting for things. We simply take a deep breath in and out to begin with to establish the connection. Then allow the breathing to continue on its own observing it for three cycles. Each cycle is an in-breath followed by an out-breath. We can observe its sound, texture, depth, duration, impact on the body or any other characteristic. Our eyes can be open or closed as we do this. If we enjoy using technology we can use a mobile app. These mini meditations can make all the difference to our mindfulness levels throughout the day.

As well as being our companion, the breath is also our protector. It protects us from suffering created by involuntary and unconscious thinking. It is not possible to be simultaneously aware of the breath and be lost in thought. Our thinking causes us problems when it is reactionary rather than responsive. Reactions are involuntary or habitual. For example, we see somebody and immediately make a judgement about him or her. A new product may be advertised and our mind immediately creates a fantasy about having the product. This is *reactive thinking*. It is involuntary and habitual. *Responsive thinking* is when we consciously choose to think out of Presence, enabling choice and creativity. This is analogous to using a tool. Let us assume we are working on a DIY project and we need to use a screwdriver. We consciously take it out of our toolbox, use it to insert a screw into a hole, and then place it back in the toolbox. We make the choice. Thinking can be practised in the same way. Once we have finished thinking, we can place it down and return to a still and peaceful state of mind. The mind becomes far more effective when it is used consciously in this way.

We are not our thoughts. How could we be? When we become aware of our thoughts, we notice that they are transient and impermanent. If we look closely at our experience, we may become aware of the awareness around and in-between the thoughts. Being aware of our thoughts means we are accessing Presence, which will guide them wisely.

When I am training groups in mindfulness, I often ask people to spend a few minutes using their phones for texting or emailing whilst keeping a small percentage of awareness on their breath. I then ask them to enter into discussions with one another using the same technique. The benefits reported include the ability to see and interpret the written word on the phone more clearly, more effective listening and the suspension of negative thoughts and judgements. This simple exercise demonstrates the power of remaining anchored to the breath.

Sexuality

Everything within our experience is influenced by Presence, and sexuality is no exception. Sexual ethics is about taking responsibility for our sexuality and using our sexual energy lovingly. This is a complex terrain covering many aspects, including thoughts, flirting, masturbation, and physical contact with others. There are two modes we use when engaging our sexuality. The first, *love-mode*, is active when we are Present. When sexuality is expressed through love, it is pleasurable, kind and generous. The second, *craving-mode*, is active when we are lost in thought. Sexual expression rooted in craving within an addictive cycle or to intoxicate the mind will always cause harm and suffering.

The subject of sexual ethics is wide enough to justify a book in its own right. Learning about the ins and outs of what is sexually ethical and what is not through reading and discussion may be helpful, but the scope and depth gained through this type of learning will always be limited. To act ethically whether it is in relation to our sexuality or any other area requires Presence. Sex is wonderful when we are Present and aware of our experience. A mind that is lost in thought during sex causes problems. Our mind can be lost in sexual thought when we are craving sex in the future or fantasizing about sex in the past. Both are forms of craving. Neither is possible at the moment of craving and we are denying the present moment, which is why we suffer. With sex, this can include a whole range of desires, including craving sexual intercourse or orgasm.

It is important to respect our human instincts and past conditioning when working with sexual ethics. For example, we may experience sexual feelings towards somebody whilst we are in an exclusive relationship. This could be due to two people being a good physical match for reproduction or it could be for some other reason. We must never judge ourself negatively for any sexual feelings or thoughts we experience. We always have an opportunity to decide how to respond to them. This is where Presence helps as it holds sexual feelings and thoughts in its awareness, allowing us to recognize them and respond wisely. Sometimes, we are caught off guard by sexual feelings, but much of the time we will know when we are entering challenging situations and can increase the intensity of our awareness to help guide us skilfully. Sexuality is an almighty force. We must be honest about our capacity to do the right thing under certain circumstances and adjust our conditions to allow for this.

Making love is a wonderful opportunity to practise being Present. This means being fully in the moment during lovemaking, being aware and accepting of our whole experience at the time, which consists of bodily sensations, form entering the senses, feelings and thoughts. Presence and lovemaking have oneness in common. When we are Present there is no ego to create a sense of self or separateness. We see ourself clearly and truthfully as being part of a universal process, connected to everybody and everything else including the person we are making love with. Making love helps to deepen our understanding of oneness by physically connecting us with our sexual partner for the duration of lovemaking. During that time, as the cells from each body are interwoven, we are physically joined and connected. Two become one. Two people are connected prior to lovemaking and will be connected subsequently as they are from the same source and part of the same universal process. Lovemaking helps us to comprehend this through a more tangible, physical arrangement of form and is a very pleasurable way of learning. If we do find that we become lost in thought during lovemaking, which is common, the practice is to simply let go of thoughts and direct our attention towards the physical experience. This is analogous to the process of dealing with distractions during meditation as described in Chapter Four. Lovemaking and any other activity that requires no thought is meditative by its nature and should be engaged with on that basis.

Masturbation can be a help or hindrance to our spiritual progression. If we are lost in thought during masturbation or intoxicated with fantasies or pornography, we will not be Present. Every time we masturbate in this way we are training the mind to escape from the present moment and enter an intoxicating dream-like state. When our body has a real need for sex, masturbation can be enjoyed and orgasm reached without using fantasy or pornography by directing our full attention to our own physical experience. This can be challenging as many of us have created an ingrained habit over the years of fantasizing to become aroused and experience orgasm. Masturbation in a state of Presence is enjoyable, free from any feelings of shame, free from harm, free from craving, and creates a wonderful positive energy.

It is offering love and attention to our bodies. Masturbating in this way creates a pleasurable meditation practising both concentration and loving kindness. This may be a gradual practice as fantasies or external stimulants are reduced over time whilst the focus on bodily sensations and sexual energy is increased.

Ideally, sexual activity including masturbation and lovemaking should be engaged with as a response to the needs of the body rather than a reaction to the wants of the mind. Some people have been conditioned to use sex as a false refuge to avoid suffering. Once we get the urge to engage in sexual activity, we may ask ourself where this is originating. If we are responding to the needs of the body and acting out of love for another or ourself, we can engage positively. If we are lost in thought, we may react to the wants of the mind and use sex to escape from unpleasant feelings such as anxiety, fear or boredom. In these instances, we have the option of becoming Present, which will enable us to respond positively and effectively to our true needs rather than using sex as an easy and ultimately ineffective way of dealing with suffering. When sex in any shape or form including masturbation, use of pornography and fantasy is used to escape from suffering, it is a form of addiction.

POINTS FOR REFLECTION

- Physical pain is experienced within the body and suffering is experienced through thought.

- The mind will not cause any stress or suffering when we are Present.

- Presence may not remove pain, but it will always remove suffering.

- A healthy body makes Presence easier to practise.

- By tuning into the body, it is possible to understand what it needs and respond accordingly.

- What our body needs may be different to what our mind craves for.

- Allowing intoxicants to enter the body causes us to become lost in thought.

- Never torment the body.

- One of the roles of the mind is to be a good servant to the body.

- Recurrent tiredness and illness are often caused through being in a constant state of resistance to what is.

- The antidote to resistance is acceptance.

- Tiredness is a manageable condition and can be experienced peacefully when it is accepted rather than resisted.

- If we have times when we are tired but it is inappropriate to rest, we can intensify our awareness or increase our concentration on an activity to create energy.

- The ego creating challenges during illness provides a golden opportunity to practise acceptance.

- If we cultivate the ability to view the body and mind as separate entities whilst acknowledging that they influence each other, we gain freedom from the suffering that is associated with bodily pain and discomfort.

- Awareness enables acceptance, which enables letting go.

- Exercise can be used as a channel to become Present as it helps us to bring awareness to the body.

- When we have some or all our attention on the breath, we are Present and connected with the here and now.

- We should take responsibility for our sexuality by expressing it lovingly.

- We should never judge ourself negatively for any sexual feelings or thoughts we have.

- Making love can be used as an opportunity to cultivate Presence.

- Sexual activity, including masturbation and lovemaking, should be engaged with as a response to the needs of the body rather than a reaction to the cravings of the mind.

OPTIONAL LEARNING ACTIVITIES

- Answer the following questions:
    - Am I eating too much or too little?
    - Am I eating what my body needs and at the right times?
    - Am I getting enough sleep?
    - Am I getting enough rest and relaxation?
    - Am I exercising too much or too little?
    - Do I have any physical conditions that need investigation?
    - Am I managing any existing physical conditions effectively?
    - Is there anything else that I can do to help my body feel well?

- The next time you are in pain, take a moment to bring awareness to it and recognize that you are the awareness, not the pain.

- Play with adjusting the intensity of exercise to cultivate your body awareness.

- Focus on your direct physical experience during masturbation or lovemaking.

- Practise anchoring a small amount of your awareness to the breath during simple activities and practise mini breathing meditations throughout the day.

- If you suffer from recurrent tiredness or illness, take steps to investigate the root causes and take action if possible.

Chapter Three

People

We can view others absolutely or relatively. In absolute terms, people do not exist and are a process of changing form in constant flux contained within a formless realm. The only thing that we can truly connect with is the formlessness within and around them. This is viewing the other person in their absolute or real state. The relative view of them is that they do exist. This relative view is a conceptual illusion created through thought. There is nothing fixed about people, but our minds need to fix and conceptualize them to make relative sense of the world and to function. What they look like, how they relate to us, their name and address, past history, possible future, our judgements about them and so on. This view is relative because it represents our mind's view of them at a point in time. In the same way, we can also view ourself relatively.

Conceptually we are all separate. We have different names, physical bodies and past experiences. Within and around all these things is something that connects us and we are all a part of it. When we connect with a person in relative terms, we are connecting through our thoughts. When we connect with a person in absolute terms, we are connecting through Presence or love, which is shared by all. Sometimes when I am in communication with people I flip between relating to them relatively with my thoughts and relating to them absolutely as a process in flux. Most people are not used to being experienced in that way. It is analogous to holding up a perfectly clear mirror to them. Temporarily, they may not be able to explain it, but they know they do not exist and have become Present. We can also apply this absolute view to ourself as well as others.

Be receptive to those who are spiritually evolved. We can make progress through connecting with the Presence they radiate. I define 'spiritually evolved' as the measure by which a person is Present. I am sure that you will recall when you have spent time with somebody and felt more alert, mindful, happier, peaceful, calmer or wiser just through being with them. You do not have to be face-to-face with a person to experience this. For example, watching a video, reading one of their books, listening to audio recordings, a telephone discussion or even bringing them to mind will have a similar effect.

Levels of Presence

As we become more Present, we naturally tune in to the level of Presence of those around us. It is like having a sixth sense. Our level of Presence varies and is influenced by the context and conditions at the time. For example, somebody may be more Present when they are in good communication with a friend compared to being around a group of people who are complaining. Our level of Presence varies according to our mental and emotional responses to what happens to us. This is an important link to keep in mind as responding positively now influences us positively in the future.

The more Present we become, the more likely it is that we are going to connect with people who are less Present than us. It is analogous to being physically fit. The fitter we become, the more people we will meet who are less fit than us. It is common for our minds to judge people as bad or complain about them, which feels unpleasant. If this happens, we simply need to be aware of it. This is a common process our minds follow to differentiate between what helps and what hinders us whilst we are learning. Once we are further along the path, the differentiation between what helps and hinders remains whilst the judgements and complaints are replaced by love and acceptance. This signifies that we have fully integrated and are living what we have learned.

We enter an upward spiral of learning how to respond appropriately to people who are living unconsciously. There is often a lag between being aware of the unskilfulness in others and being able to respond appropriately at the time. As our awareness grows, there may be certain challenges relating to people who cause us to react, allowing the unskilfulness of others to trigger unskilfulness within us. In order to respond positively and kindly to another who is being unskilful, our level of Presence needs to be much higher than theirs. This applies, even more, when we are in communication with a group of people who are collectively behaving unskilfully. Our ability to stay Present fluctuates significantly dependent upon our conditions, so we must watch out for labelling others or ourself as being 'more evolved' or 'spiritually superior' because until people are fully awakened, their state can be changed in an instant.

As long as our level of Presence is sufficiently high when in the company of others either on a one-to-one basis or in groups, we will respond wisely regardless of our knowledge of the situation at the time. The opposite is also true in that if we are lost in thought, we can count on causing harm to ourself or others in some shape or form even if only on a subtle level. When we are lost in thought, we lose touch with who we really are.

Love & Control

Some religions have lists that point to skilfulness and unskilfulness. For example, Buddhism has precepts and Christianity has commandments. Understanding and following training principles such as being generous, telling the truth, not causing harm and so on can be a real help. These lists are especially helpful to those who experienced an absence of ethical guidance in childhood. One of the many benefits of being Present is that right action follows regardless of our conscious knowledge of what right is. This is in the form of thoughts, speech or physical action. Presence provides a connection to the wisdom that transcends our conscious thinking and enables us to respond with love. Wisdom comes from seeing clearly and through seeing clearly we see that we are not separate from others in absolute terms. It is through this understanding of non-separateness that love flows.

One can describe the opposite to love as control, which originates from the ego. Control is based upon attachment and craving. What creates and sustains the ego is the delusion of seeing ourself, everybody and everything else as separate. We only create attachments in relation to people and things when we believe they are separate from us. When we understand that everything and everybody is connected, we see that trying to control a mentally constructed fantasy link between us and whatever we are attached to is futile, delusional and leads to suffering. Aversion or craving also assumes that what is out there is separate and that we must move towards or away from it. This is trying to control what is ultimately uncontrollable.

It is problematic when the ego tries to control things or people, because the control is always rooted in fear. Essentially, this is the fear of losing the false sense of self, which defines the ego. However, it is fine to set intentions based on love and positive needs. If you desire a particular outcome and you believe that outcome would be positively beneficial, you can set an intention. If the outcome is what the universe requires and the conditions are right, it will come about without you trying to control things. I have experienced this many times in the past. I set a positive intention for a person (including myself) or situation where I want something to happen or not to happen. I then actively let go of trying to control things and as if by magic, what I want is manifested. This is a lot about trusting that things will go in the direction they are meant to go and having the confidence to take our hands off the steering wheel, allowing the universal process of evolving consciousness to do the driving. On the surface, intentions appear powerful. The power is not really in the intention, but in the wisdom that informs it, and the wisdom is informed through seeing clearly. When we set an intention based upon what is actually needed, it will have the illusion of manifesting based upon the intention rather than the fact that it was always meant to be. Positive intentions and wishes which are based on love are a symbol of Presence, an alignment with what is, and what needs to be.

Knowing Our Triggers

It can appear that some people 'push our buttons' causing us to react unskilfully. The people who trigger these reactions within us are often those we are close to, such as our partners, good friends and family members. Sometimes, when we are lost in thought, it can feel as though anybody is capable of pushing our buttons. To start with, we may be unaware that we are reacting at all. We blame and label those involved as 'difficult people'. People can remind one another of old issues they have not fully resolved and push their buttons, triggering difficult emotions. This can be unplanned or a deliberate attempt from one ego to trigger the other. Over time and as our awareness grows, it allows us to see the causes and effects and that this type of reactivity is something that we must take responsibility for.

In *A New Earth*[4], Eckhart Tolle used the analogy of a dimmer switch turning up the power within his body and he remained intensely Present in the company of an agitated neighbour with a strong ego. I use this analogy to help me when interacting with people I find difficult. The dimmer switch on my internal light is increased to its highest setting and the wisdom that is enabled through that light allows me to respond with love. The right response, which is appropriate at that point in time, emanates naturally. It could be something physical that we do or something we communicate. It may even be walking away or remaining still and silent. If the other person is lost in their thoughts and reacting in a way that is harmful, they will be harming themselves. We can be harmed physically, but do not need to be harmed psychologically, as we are immune from unskilful thoughts and emotional reactions when we are Present.

Through intensification of Presence, we are using the energy from the difficult situation positively in the same way that a martial arts expert uses the energy from an opponent to defeat them. What we are defeating here is not an opponent or situation, but our own ego.

Creating Space & Letting Go

The vision is to be fully Present with everybody we spend time with. Prior to being awakened, we may find ourself reacting to some people despite our best efforts. In these cases, it may be necessary to remove ourself from their company or reduce the amount of time we spend with them. I had to make this decision with my parents. After trying my best, I had to accept that when I was in communication with them my level of Presence was not high enough for me to contain my reactivity. The resulting thoughts and actions created a great deal of emotional pain and suffering. I decided to create some space from them for a while, allowing me to let go of old thinking habits relating to my childhood, which were causing the reactions. Some people judged me to begin with. Once I explained the situation, they understood that my intentions were positive and accepted the decision. We have to be careful not to get caught up in any feelings of irrational guilt in these situations and remind ourself of our positive intentions. A while later, after using the time and space to heal, I was able to be Present in my parents' company and respond lovingly to any reactions I experienced. Decisions to create space or let go of relationships need careful consideration. This is especially true if they are close relationships, including those with family members, partners and good friends. If we create space or let go through a reaction when we are lost in thought, we will be acting with the intention of control rather than love.

When we choose to let go of a relationship or create space, we must be prepared for the possibility of experiencing a sense of loss. Letting go of a dysfunctional relationship is letting go of a part of our ego if it identifies with the dysfunction. It can be spiritually beneficial and at the same time uncomfortable. This can happen in abusive relationships. The abuser identifies with abusing and the abused identifies with being the subject of abuse. Both of these identifications are created and sustained by their respective egos.

It is natural that as we become more Present, we will have a very different outlook on personal relationships and friendship. Both will lean more towards cultivating Presence through communication, which may also be referred to as spiritual friendship. Gaps created as we let go of dysfunctional personal relationships or friendships may take a little time to fill with something more conducive if indeed they need filling at all. This is all part of the journey.

'Difficult' People & Situations

From time to time we enter into situations involving people we find difficult. A natural tendency here can be to loop around our thoughts, trying to find the reasons why this person is the way they are, why we reacted to them and what needs to be done to 'fix' the situation. Accompanying the ruminating thoughts are often judgements and a multitude of unpleasant feelings such as anger, resentment, frustration or anxiety. Whether we do this alone or with others, it makes for a very unpleasant and tiring form of analysis that uses speculation in an attempt to deduce the reasons for the person not meeting our expectations. This approach to resolving things creates more difficulty than it solves. Some problems are too complex for our minds to solve and more often than not we do not have all the facts. There is a far easier and effective way to work through these situations, which is to face the person and situation with Presence moment-by-moment. If our ego has an expectation about how we think somebody should be, craving and suffering will follow. We crave for them to be a certain way and then suffer if they do not meet our expectations. Meaning, judging and complaining about others are always underpinned by ego-formed expectations. Strictly speaking, it is our ego that is judging and complaining, not our true self. The amount that people complain out loud or in their thoughts says a lot about how much they are evolved spiritually. Our true self accepts everyone as they are now and everything as it is now.

When we encounter a difficult person, it is helpful to acknowledge our opinions and beliefs and be open to them being invalid. For example, we may have believed that somebody was angry about something we had done, but this belief might not have been based upon any direct evidence. So we had formed an opinion about them. The person in question may well have been angry about something we had done, but at that point in time, we did not know for sure. Our job is to observe and transcend our own thoughts rather than becoming lost in them and proliferating. Everything within our experience must be accepted fully, including the fact that we have opinions and at the same time, we may not know for sure what the real truth is. We are not our thoughts and opinions, but the awareness that observes them. Realizing this enables us to transcend our thoughts and draw upon a far richer source of wisdom that will give us everything we need to guide us through any difficult situation regardless of whether we have all the facts. Ideally, when we communicate with people, we stay Present. The communication can take any form, including physical actions, verbal communication, reading or writing. One of the easiest ways to do this is to anchor a small amount of our awareness to the breath during the communication.

We must try not to get lost in our own beliefs and opinions and be open about the possibility that we do not know. Surrendering to not knowing and knowing that there is no guarantee we will ever know is the way. I recall a time when I was driving with my son. I asked how many hours he needed to do his homework over the weekend to get him thinking ahead so that he could schedule the time required to complete it. His response was, "I don't know" and that was all he said to begin with. He was telling the truth. At that point in time he did not know. When I asked him again a minute or so later, he provided an answer. It sometimes works like that. Acknowledging the fact that we do not know enables the mind to find the answer.

At some point in the future, we may know the true reasons about why a difficult person behaved the way they did, but that is irrelevant as part of this practice. What is important here is to observe what our thoughts are doing, keep an open mind to the truth of the situation and cultivate Presence. The practice of bringing awareness to our beliefs, being open to not knowing, resting in the facts of the situation and cultivating Presence can be applied to any situation regardless of whether it involves people. Out of the Presence that is created through seeing a situation clearly flows love. The love is integrated with a sense of connectedness to our true self, others and everything else involved in the situation. It is a magical phenomenon that transforms our problems and difficulties into clarity and creativity.

We may connect indirectly with people who are suffering and find it difficult to be around them. If we are lost in thought, we may react and see these people and their behaviour as a problem to us. If we are Present, we respond with acceptance, compassion and a wish for them to be happy. I have often experienced this in restaurants. Whilst eating a meal and being lost in thought, I found myself getting irritated at anybody who I perceived to be disturbing my peace such as people complaining, troubled children or staff who did not conform to my service expectations. When I am Present, it is quite the opposite. Acceptance, compassion and well-wishing flow freely.

If we are around people who are unskilful in their speech or actions, we either remain in their company or we leave. The decision to stay or leave needs to take our own level of Presence into account. If we are confident that we can remain Present in the face of their unskilfulness, then staying around may help them become more Present and transform the situation. If we feel we are at risk of becoming lost in thought and then acting unskilfully ourselves, we should consider moving away. Our ability to be in the company of those less Present than ourself and remain skilful depends upon the difference between our level of Presence and theirs at the time. This is always subject to change and needs to be gauged throughout the duration of the time spent with a person or a group of people.

I use this method when I occasionally attend meals on an evening involving alcohol. Generally speaking, my energy levels are higher in the morning and dip as the evening progresses. Often the situation is such that I am not drinking alcohol and everybody else is. At the start of the evening, I can be Present. Later on in the evening, there is a point where I feel tired, making it easier for me to become lost in thought. In parallel with this, the level of Presence of those around me lowers as more alcohol is consumed. There is a certain tipping point in the evening where I know that I will become overwhelmed and lose my ability to remain Present if I stay there so I choose to make a polite exit beforehand, ensuring that I am both skilful in the evening and refreshed in the morning. Being Present around people who are unskilful helps you understand them without judgement as their faults will be more visible, allowing you to get to know them more.

It is possible to be with people who we find unpleasant without suffering. It is quite normal to find people unpleasant or dislike them. It is not the person we dislike, but their attributes that conflict with what we are attached to, including our expectations about them. We react when our expectations are not met. For example, if we expect our supervisor or manager to promote us and that does not happen, we can make them a difficult person in our minds. It is fine to have preferences, but once the preference turns into an attachment or identification, suffering is sure to follow. The ego uses our preferences to create attachments when we are lost in thought. Preferences in themselves are fine. It is the attachment to those preferences that cause the problems and suffering.

Unpleasant thoughts and feelings are created and this causes us to suffer. Behind the unskilfulness lies the true essence of the person. Trying to convince ourself that we should like something about somebody we do not like and judging ourself as a result of this is futile. We can love people who have attributes that we do not like and we love them by seeing beyond our ego and theirs. They have been created as part of the same universal process and are simply responding to their past conditioning. Some of their conditions led them to say or do things that cause us to react. We find their actions unpleasant because of our own past conditioning. A tension is created and we either get lost in thought, which causes problems, or we become aligned and peaceful by bringing Presence into the situation.

When people judge us, the real issue has nothing to do with us. It is related to something they need to work on. If somebody is judging us, it means that they are failing to accept their experience about us. Therefore, they are judging themselves. They can never accept us. Acceptance does not work like that. Acceptance is an internal process which takes place within the person who is doing the accepting. They must accept their own personal experience in relation to others. For example, if we say something that somebody finds unpleasant, they have to accept their own unpleasant feelings. When somebody judges us, they are in a state of resistance and think we should be different to what we actually are at that point in time to allow them to feel okay. However we are judged, when we are Present, we respond appropriately. We see that the person is actually judging his or her own experience and not us. It may not be an enjoyable experience for us, but our mind will be peaceful.

We can allow challenges with people to help us make spiritual progress just like we can lift weights to build muscle. If we find ourself suffering and in a state of resistance with difficult people, the first step should be to try and bring acceptance to our feelings about them. The suffering and resistance we experience is a calling to try harder to love them. To try harder to love them, we must try harder to stay Present. When we are Present, we can see clearly, removing the separateness between others and ourself, which opens up the channel for love. This is what true love really is.

Understanding and honesty about who we can spend time with and for how long without harming ourself allows us to manage our conditions so they are more conducive to staying Present. Difficult people are pre-selected and presented to us without having to work to find them. We should never knowingly create enemies or challenges. We can allow them to manifest naturally. The challenge faced will always be a product of the unskilfulness of the people we are with, the amount of time we spend with them and how lost in thought we are at the time. It is impossible to be compromised by the actions of others when we are Present, because there is nobody there to be compromised. Only the ego can be compromised and the ego and Presence cannot coexist. When we are Present, there is a deep knowing that there is no absolute separateness between us and everybody else. We can see the ego operating in others and at the same time be able to connect with their true essence, which is sacred and shared with the true essence of us. This is how we love others and are able to accept and deal with any surface-level challenges they create for us.

We must establish a principle to focus on our own unskilfulness rather than on the unskilfulness of others. This is empowering and a better use of our energy as we have more influence to correct ourself. It also helps free us up from gossiping, slanderous speech, judgements and derogatory thoughts. People may raise concerns about others in their own minds or in conversation to enable them to feel superior. A large ego and personal insecurity are often the underlying causes of this. When we judge others, we are judging ourself. If we turn our attention inwards, we may find that the unskilfulness we are using in our judgements is actually within us. This is often the case when we think that we have corrected our unskilfulness in a given area, but unbeknown to us there is some residue remaining. People who have recently given up smoking will often do this and judge other smokers for a while as they are still releasing their own addiction. When we judge, we are judging our own experience, never the other person. If somebody does something we do not agree with and we have unpleasant feelings or negative thoughts about them, we are actually judging our own feelings or thoughts. We then conceptually project that judgement onto the other person, creating a sense of separateness and refusing to take responsibility for how we feel or what we think. When we truly accept how we feel and what we think, we may then feel that we are accepting the other person albeit conceptually.

Presence through Communication

Most of us have numerous opportunities on a daily basis to practise being Present whilst in communication with others. Just a small amount of contact is enough to practise and space in-between communication can be used for reflection. If we are Present during communication with others, our behaviours and speech will be truthful, kind and harmonious, responding to whatever is required at the time. This is regardless of how 'intelligent' we are or how much we know about a given situation or person. A by-product of this type of communication, which in some cases may be silence, is that we may teach those who are receptive. This way of teaching is far more effective than guessing at what people might need and advising them. In this case, it is not really us who are teaching them. What is teaching them is Presence or the truth, with our form identity as the conduit. A true spiritual teacher will never force advice or opinions onto others or be identified with their role as a teacher.

It can be helpful to reflect on our communication with others asking self-directed questions such as, "was I Present during that communication?" or "did I manage to stay anchored to my breath whilst I was with them?" A useful indicator that we have been lost in thought is when we experience shame during or after communication due to thinking, saying or doing something unskilful. Examples can be hateful thoughts, or slanderous or dishonest speech. Once we become Present after the communication, we wake up and realize our faults. If there were faults within the communication, we can be sure that we were lost in thought and there is an opportunity to reflect further and learn what we need to do differently next time.

Through communication with others, we may experience a variety of pleasant and unpleasant feelings. A discussion with a friend about something we are looking forward to may trigger a feeling of excitement. We will experience pleasurable feelings through spending time with somebody we find beautiful. If our path crosses with an enemy, this may trigger feelings of resentment or anger. Whoever we are in communication with, it is likely that feelings will be created. The person we are in communication with does not control our feelings although it may feel like that sometimes. Our feelings are our reactions to the stimulus created through the communication. Even without being on the holiday we are excited about, the anticipated feelings can be created through the visualization. The whole process is very reactive and automatic when we are lost in thought. It is important not to judge these feelings when they arise. We should bring awareness and acceptance to them. We can experience feelings and acknowledge them with brief internal dialogue such as "there is a feeling of excitement", "there is a feeling of anger", "there is a pleasant feeling" or "there is an unpleasant feeling". Judging feelings through additional internal or external dialogue, labelling them, as good, bad, criticising and feeling guilty are all unnecessary, and lead to being lost in thought. Our practice is to simply acknowledge and let go of each feeling as it enters our awareness.

During our communication with others, we may experience thoughts. For example, a friend may be telling us about something great they achieved and before they have finished speaking, we may already be lost in thought, thinking of how we could achieve the same. Another example is when somebody is sharing a problem with us and we are lost in thought thinking about a solution before they have finished communicating. Again, this is all very reactive. There will be no Presence and quality in those thoughts and whatever results from them. Whilst all this is going on, our thoughts are causing problems, as they will always be unskilful in some shape or form if we are unaware of them. The opposite is true and thoughts that are manifested through Presence are skilful. When we are lost in thought, we can fail to listen fully and miss the opportunity to connect.

True communication is Presence in one person connecting with Presence in another. Presence is shared and what is actually happening is that it is communicating with itself, which it delights in. The forms of the two people are enabling a channel for wisdom and love to flow. This is why it feels so good when you are in true communication with another person. During this time, the ego is inactive, which means no dysfunction and suffering. We can meet somebody for the first time and communicate in this way. It feels like that person is an old friend who we have enjoyed time with before. The two people may not have met previously, but Presence has most certainly flowed in this way for both of them beforehand, which is why the experience feels familiar. Spiritual friendship is manifested when people are Present through true communication. It helps our practice to honour and cultivate these types of friendships. The opposite of true communication is false communication, which is where the egos of both people are connecting and feeding each other. Be aware that the feelings that accompany false communication may feel pleasurable at times, despite them hindering us.

Communication is wider than just face-to-face contact and includes, but is not limited to, telephone discussions, emails, text messages and social media. Every touch-point with another person is a form of communication. For all forms of communication, we can make a conscious decision to sustain Presence throughout the interactions.

True Listening

The majority of children are provided with instruction and support from their parents and teachers in the areas of speaking, reading, writing, mathematics and a range of other skills. What surprises me is that children have little or no instruction or support with listening. Many people go through their whole lives without any guidance on how to listen to others. Listening is essential to our development and a key ingredient in meaningful relationships. True listening is to listen to another person whilst being Present. When we truly listen, we are fully receptive, taking on board helpful information without judgement and discarding what is irrelevant or has the potential to hinder us.

True listening results in learning and progress as we retain useful information and are able to recall it as and when required to help respond creatively to future situations. This is the case regardless of the channel for listening, which includes listening to somebody you are with in person, listening on the phone, reading a message, listening to audio, reading a book or listening to somebody talking on the TV. With true listening, there is a deep concentration that provides the energy to keep us alert and focused. People we are listening to may also become Present as they follow our example. They will feel heard, accepted and loved. We can provide them with a clear mirror that reflects back what they are communicating and helps them to bring awareness to the feelings that are present within them at the time. We give them attention, which is a basic human need. The whole interaction is progressive and generous.

The word 'listening' is often used to refer to what we hear. True listening transcends traditional listening. True listening concentrates on the spoken word and is also aware of everything else coming in through the senses, including body language from the person speaking and our own internal feelings, thoughts and compulsions. This enables us to experience the communication holistically, including our internal reactions and allows us access to the intentions behind what is being communicated. True listening involves being connected to the formless realm whilst being aware of form entering the senses and our internal experience. One way that the connection with the formless can be enabled is through being aware of the silence between sounds and the space between objects. The formless realm is another way of describing Presence.

False listening is communication entering our senses whilst we are lost in thought. During these times, the ego may temporarily trick ourself or the other person into believing that we are truly listening. The lack of awareness prevalent in false listening means that we are at risk of missing or discarding helpful information and retaining information that hinders us. False listening always leads to harm in some shape or form. It is a way of stealing time and energy from people as they offer us communication, which we pay little or no attention to. False listening may lead to the person communicating becoming confused or unskilful as our absence of Presence may also lead to them becoming lost in thought.

Even when we can truly listen to somebody consistently, our listening can deepen further. This is because true listening is led by Presence and Presence is a continuum that deepens with practice. It is for these reasons that for most of us, true listening is a lifelong practice which can be used to cultivate Presence in everyday life. Most people get plenty of opportunities to practise this through being with other people or engaging in another form of listening such as reading.

Fortunately, there is a range of techniques that we can deploy to truly listen to somebody. These techniques are simple to understand and often difficult to practise. If it is possible at the time of listening, we should keep our body still. A still body helps to cultivate a still mind and a still mind is what is required for true listening. An exception to this rule would be if a friend was speaking whilst we were walking and stillness was not possible. Our posture whilst listening should represent a balance of alertness and relaxation. A body that is overly alert or energized can trigger distracting thoughts and a body that is too relaxed can cause us to become sleepy and daydream. So whilst sitting or standing, we keep our back straight and shoulders relaxed. The guidance for the body here is identical to the guidance offered in formal meditation, because true listening is a form of meditation. Our eyes should be softly focused on the person we are listening to. We should avoid staring intensely, as this will distract the person talking.

The listening becomes a meditation. As we listen, we can anchor a small amount of attention to the breath. This technique, which I reference many times, will keep us grounded in the present moment. If we prefer, we can use a part of the body as a substitute for the breath, including awareness of the energy within our hands or feet. As we listen we may find that other external and internal form objects enter our field of awareness. People may be passing by; we may hear their voices and conversations. We may experience other distractions from the environment. This is all fine and our response is identical to that of formal meditation. We direct our attention back to the person speaking, which is our object of concentration, allowing the distraction to pass in its own time. This practice of returning to the focus of concentration may need to be repeated many times during the communication, dependent upon the amount of distraction we experience. An exception to this would be if something urgent needed our attention that justified an interruption.

As a person is speaking, we may experience a multitude of feelings including excitement, happiness, anxiety and so on. As these feelings come into awareness, we acknowledge them, allow them to be and allow them to pass. The same goes with our own thoughts that we become aware of as we listen. Any internal or external distraction that we are aware of needs to be accepted; allowed to be and allowed to pass. Some of the thoughts may be of a judgemental or comparative nature. This is the ego's way of trying to reinforce a false sense of separateness between us and the other person. It leads to us seeing other people based on our own projected view of them rather than who they truly are. We should not judge ourself for judging as this adds more judgement, increases thinking and strengthens the ego. If judgements do arise when listening to others, we can simply let them go.

We make judgements about people or situations because our egos have expectations about how things are or should be. It is natural to make judgements, as our minds are trying to make sense of the world based upon our past experiences and conditioning. We must be aware of our judgements and see them in their true perspective, which is that they are based on our own limited knowledge and experience. This awareness differentiates a person who is making conscious judgements from a person who is being unconsciously judgemental. If we are aware of our judgements and hold them in perspective, any action we take, including speech, will utilize that same perspective and be wiser as a result.

At times, when we are listening to somebody, we may interrupt him or her. Interruptions are fine if they are made consciously, which will mean the motivation for the interruption is wise and considered. If we interrupt people unconsciously, we will not be aware of the interruption at the time, which means we will not be aware of its motive. We may be aware of the interruption after, through reflection or somebody pointing it out to us. Unconscious interruptions are problematic. This is a sneaky tactic used by the ego that is always based on craving and control. Unpleasant feelings after interruption are feedback mechanisms from the body telling us that the ego has reacted.

Occasionally I will consciously interrupt people. This usually happens at work if I have a time constraint. I am confident that somebody is going down a blind alley in a work-based discussion or taking a disproportionate amount of time in a meeting, I may choose to stop them through the use of interruption. This type of interruption feels fine afterwards and has never caused a problem to anybody else, to the best of my knowledge. If I consciously interrupt, I will sometimes follow up with the person I interrupted shortly after and explain my motives. Conscious interruptions should always be made from a place of Presence, as they require wisdom to be used effectively and kindly.

After listening to somebody without interruption, it can be helpful to leave a gap before we respond. This gap or silence lasting from a fraction of a second to several minutes provides an opportunity for both people's minds to become still. When we are communicating with Presence, we know exactly what is required at the time, which may be verbal communication, body language, stillness, silence or a combination of all four. Thinking about what to communicate is not required when you are Present as the response will be creative and spontaneous. It is unreasonable to expect the thinking mind to determine how and what to communicate for the best, as situations involving others are far too complex. When we are lost in thought, our responses will be reactive and we will follow a path based on our past experiences. Most of the time the reactions will be inappropriate or sub-optimal. For example, if we have a habit of smiling when we are nervous or laughing when we are confused, we will do that. If we have a habit of saying "yes" whenever we are asked to do something, we will do that. The problem with this reactive approach is that it assumes that things are fixed and that old patterns serve future situations. The truth is that every moment is completely fresh and deserves to be served by a creative response accessible only through a state of Presence.

Early in my career, I interrupted people in the office most of the time without even being aware that I was doing it. I would interrupt people regularly in one-to-one discussions and meetings in an attempt to put forward my opinions and control situations. I wanted to control[5] things because I was attached to the money I was earning and afraid about what might happen should I lose my job. When somebody else was talking, I would be thinking about what I was going to say next or how I could interrupt them, instead of listening. This proved to be limiting and also irritated people! It was difficult to build quality relationships and I was unable to work collaboratively with others. Anything that I created or delivered was limited as it was a result of my own views and opinions rather than working with others to produce better results together.

After a few months of being in the job, I had this issue brought to my attention by my line manager within a performance review. It came as quite a shock to me and after some investigation, it turned out that the majority of the people I worked with had the opinion that I did not listen or give them space to put forward their views. Subsequent to this, I was assigned a coach to help me resolve the issue. He gave me a great tip. He told me that I should mentally count to three after somebody had finished speaking before I responded to ensure I did not interrupt. I did what he recommended and those gaps felt like they lasted a lifetime to start with. At first, during each gap, I would become concerned that if I waited too long before speaking, I would never be heard and lose my opportunity to contribute. What I was really afraid of was losing control. As it turned out, the technique did work well and helped me to listen and allow others to finish speaking before making my points. Over time and with practice, relationships improved and I became more collaborative, which met the needs of the organization and my colleagues. These days, I do not count to three every time somebody has finished speaking, but I still try to observe a brief pause, which is a great helper for sustaining or regaining Presence during communication.

Solitude & Loneliness

Our practice needs to integrate time spent alone and time spent with others. People often complain about feeling lonely. Loneliness is triggered by thoughts that work on the invalid assumption that we are separate from everybody and everything else. The delusion of loneliness is enabled by the delusion of separateness. The deeper we understand the truth that we are part of a universal process of conditions and that the true essence of us is connected with everybody and everything else, the less we feel lonely. Believing in loneliness also disempowers us from understanding and taking responsibility for meeting our own needs. We may find limiting beliefs that are linking certain conditions to our concept of loneliness. For example, one person may feel lonely if they are home during a weekend when they expect to be out with their friends. Another may be identified with being the centre of attention and feel lonely in a group if they have not been communicated with for a few minutes. The delusion of loneliness can manifest in many situations, dependent upon how the concept is viewed by the individual. If we find ourself on our own then we are meant to be alone at that point in time. That is an essential part of our journey and evolution. The concept of loneliness is unnecessarily added by our ego when we are in resistance to what is and craving for things to be different.

Bringing awareness to feelings associated with our concept of loneliness is helpful. We can use them as a feedback mechanism to trigger awareness and understanding of the thought patterns and dysfunction that lies beneath. If we are unaware of loneliness, we will react unskilfully and might complain or lean on our addictions for comfort or escape. Another sign of somebody trying to escape from their unpleasant feelings is that they become desperate to connect with others, purely to move away from their own suffering. They are connecting from a place of believing they are separate, which feels unauthentic to the recipient. To add to the suffering, people who initiate these types of neurotic connections may also create attachments to those who respond. Giving our full attention to unpleasant feelings and emotional pain is the only way that they can be sustainably reduced and ultimately released. This is how healing takes place. Escaping from the emotional pain will feed and sustain it. As our ego dissolves, so does our belief in loneliness. The more we progress, the more we see clearly that who we really are is never really alone. This clarity enables us to spend time alone in peace, which is true solitude. We can feel connected and harmonious with people regardless of whether they are physically with us. This connectivity and harmoniousness is another way of describing love.

Periods of solitude are particularly advantageous when we have times around people who are lost in thought and behaving unconsciously. Being around these people can trigger hindrances within us, which lead to us being lost in thought too. The more we progress, the easier it will be for us to stay Present around others. We must know our limitations though and consider whom we should be around and for how long. Solitude provides an opportunity to become still and spacious. We can work with our own internal hindrances without the additional hindrances of others distracting us. These sacred times allow us to reconnect with who we are, which puts us in a strong position to re-engage with others.

Friendship

Friends map onto one of three types at any given time. The first type is the 'Wise Friend'. The wise friend is, generally speaking, more Present than we are, although in certain situations this may change temporarily. The second type of friend is the 'Aspiring Friend' who is, generally speaking, less Present than us. This type of friend is receptive and wants to learn from us. Despite them getting lost in thought more of the time than we do, when we are with them, their level of Presence increases. We inspire and support the aspiring friend. The third type of friend is the 'Spiritual Peer'. The spiritual peer is at a similar level to us in terms of their general level of Presence whilst we may observe variances in certain situations. Spiritual peers are valuable as they meet the qualities of wise and aspiring friends. They inspire and support each other.

I have introduced the friendship types to help you understand that spiritual friendship can exist with people at all levels. These three types of friendships represent 'True Friendship'. True friendship, which may also be known as spiritual friendship, actively supports the cultivation of Presence. True friendship plays a significant part in the human race becoming more conscious.

It is helpful if friends have an intellectual understanding of spiritual teachings, but not essential. There are vast numbers of people who are Present much of the time, but may not be able to point to it intellectually in the same way as a teacher or a book might. The primary connection between two people who are true friends is always Presence, which can also be described as love. After true friends have spent time together, they feel nourished and experience pleasant feelings such as gratitude and appreciation as a result of the good that has been done through their communication and action. The formless connection links them regardless of where they are located and when they last made contact. If they are apart and not in direct communication, it can feel as though they are still connected. This is because they experienced Presence within an earlier connection with each other and they are experiencing Presence again albeit in a different context. They believe the connection is with each other as it feels the same. It is with each other and also with everybody and everything else.

The opposite of true friendship is false friendship. False friendship actively hinders the cultivation of Presence. We find that these friendships, which are not true friendships, are built upon a dysfunctional platform. For example, this could be people who hang out together to get intoxicated or spend time gossiping or complaining. They could be people who come together purely for pleasure that they both crave for. After false friends have spent time together, if they are sufficiently aware, they will feel depleted and experience unpleasant feelings such as shame or resentment as a result of the harm caused by their actions.

True friendship and false friendship are actually modes rather than fixed relationships between people. The reality of most relationships is that they will contain attributes that help and hinder us. Whatever impact one friend has on another is reciprocated. This means that if we help a friend, we will be helping ourself. If we hinder a friend, we will be hindering ourself. For example, if we help a friend through being very aware and listening to what they have to say, we will benefit from manifesting that awareness. If we are distracted whilst our friend is telling us something, this will hinder us as well as hindering our friend's ability to communicate. This phenomenon illustrates how we are all connected and demonstrates the breadth of the impact our state of being has on ourself, those we connect with, and ultimately the universe.

It may help to conceptually label friends as wise friends, aspiring friends, spiritual peers and false friends, but remember that these are just concepts and modes of communication at a point in time. These concepts can help us to navigate our way around friendship and to understand how our network of friends impacts our practice. Every communication between two people will be in one of two modes at any point in time: true friendship or false friendship. People are not fixed and any spiritual maturity comparison should only be taken relatively, on the understanding that it is conceptual rather than real. Even during a brief discussion or meeting, the mode of friendship can change as two people enter into and out of a state of Presence multiple times.

We may have a friend who feels like a spiritual peer until they become unskilful through their addictions. If we can stay Present during these times, bringing awareness to the physical sensations in our body, our feelings and thoughts, this will have a therapeutic effect on our friend's underlying pain, helping to reduce or release it. It is for this reason that when we are Present it can be helpful if friends unintentionally trigger emotional pain. Friends who push our buttons without a conscious intention to do so can be seen as helpers as long as we remain Present at the time and are aware of the pain caused. Awareness of the pain means that we are starving the ego rather than feeding it. It is always the ego that triggers emotional pain. True friendships and personal relationships are a process of unknowingly triggering emotional pain whilst being available, understanding, supportive and Present for one another.

Activities within true friendship are relatively unimportant as long as they are not causing harm, as the primary benefit of the communication is spiritual progress. True friendship gives both parties the option of pointing out when the other is lost in thought to help bring them back into the present moment. They might ask each other, "Are you lost in thought right now?" or "Are you Present?" These questions activate awareness, encourage friends to transcend thought and raise their level of consciousness.

Regardless of what people might say, any type of friendship is based on an exchange of meeting needs. It may sound clinical, but that is how it is. Two people become friends because they can serve each other in some way. The whole landscape of a friendship will change over time, which in turn changes the impact it will have on the friends being Present together. Over time, needs change and it may be that some friendships are no longer helpful in their previous form. As our needs change, we find the dynamics of existing friendships changing. These dynamics include the frequency of time we spend together and the activities we get involved in. We may also need new friends. This can happen at an exponential rate as people get onto the spiritual path. If we let go of spending time with old friends, we can still love them and be open to serving them in the future. Serving a friend can be as simple as bringing Presence into communication or spending time together in silence. New friendships have the benefit of freshness. Often, a new friend may know very little about our past and therefore may be able to accept us for who we are now without mentally referring back to who we once were. Any friend, new or old, can do this at any time when they are Present because the present moment does not involve time. It only involves now.

It is wise to be aware of how our current friendships are impacting us. If required, we should make changes to whom we spend time with, where we spend time with them and the frequency in which we meet. If we are Present, this will happen spontaneously and require little thought. That said, for most of us, it is worth taking time out on a regular basis to consciously think through the situation with our various friendships and make any necessary adjustments after careful consideration.

Changes to Personal Relationships

People may experience changes within personal relationships as they become more Present. Some relationships support our spiritual practice, some require changes and others need to end. I was in a relationship with my wife at the time for sixteen years and the majority of those were happy and beneficial. My ex-wife is a kind, beautiful woman and a wonderful mother. The communication and intimacy within the relationship dissipated and I knew deep within myself that I needed to let go. I knew that things needed to change, but did not know the reasons why. Now that I look back and connect the dots, I can identify the reasons. I have also been involved in other relationships which I knowingly let go of. I was conscious enough to spot the dysfunction and hindrances, did my best to resolve them at the time and then let go, being fully conscious of my decisions and justi-fication. When we are in touch with who we really are, we will always know what to do, but may not always know why we must do it.

In many cases, personal relationships come with attachments. Tradi-tional romance-formed straight relationships can lead to the creation of strong bi-directional dependencies, which is nature's way of keeping two people together to reproduce and nurture children who will transcend them. Both sides will be dependent on the relationship for things they may not be confident providing for themselves. This can be based upon pleasure or deficiencies of somebody that are being plugged by the coun-tering strengths of their partner. Somebody who is often depressed may feel better when in a relationship with somebody who is usually happy. Somebody who is lazy by nature may operate more effectively in a rela-tionship with a more active partner. Somebody who has low self-esteem may feel better if they are in a relationship with somebody who accepts them and rejoices in their strengths and talents. These dependencies can be created even if the two people are unable to have children due to age, gender or medical reasons.

The dependencies are a form of attachment. With attachment comes grasping and craving, which are both unhelpful. With progress, the need for this type of dysfunctional personal relationship dissipates as people become happier and able to get their needs met without being dependent and attached. The dysfunctional relationship can be replaced with a happy single life or a spiritual relationship. A spiritual relationship provides many of the benefits that come with a romantic personal relationship with the additional benefit of helping both parties to become more Present. These relationships contain both lightness and skilfulness. The lightness comes from the fact that there is much less attachment. The pleasurable feelings that are part and parcel of romance can be enjoyed and held in awareness whilst experiencing freedom from the associated attachments. There may well be dependencies in place, but both parties will be aware and accepting of them. The dependencies may even be openly discussed on a regular basis. The skilfulness is channelled from the wisdom that is created through the partners bringing Presence into the relationship.

Both partners may be committed to each other and at the same time can let go of the relationship if that is what is required for them to evolve. If they do let go, they know they can confidently hold any related suffering in a field of awareness and love. This makes them far less vulnerable and more confident within the relationship. There is an appreciation that the suffering is relative because the primary factor in their life is Presence. Spiritual relationships represent a middle way for those who are taking their practice seriously whilst wanting to enjoy the benefits of a partner. Spaciousness and acceptance in various forms will feature highly in these relationships, as will other critical ingredients for practice.

It is common that one person within a relationship outgrows the other spiritually. In fact, it is inevitable as no two people are in exactly the same place and evolve at the same rate. Outgrowing another person spiritually in this context means being more Present than them for more of the time. In many relationships, this gap is manageable and can help both partners develop. In some cases, the gap is unmanageable and it becomes a hindrance to their practice. If it is unmanageable and not possible to make changes to allow the gap to exist harmoniously, then the relationship will need to end. This is sad to experience or observe as it often creates suffering in the lead-up and subsequent to the separation. It is more common in younger couples due to a faster acceleration of spiritual progress in most cases. I have intuitively been able to sense this in friends' relationships on a number of occasions. I can see clearly that one person is progressing much faster than the other and that the gap is widening. This often happens if one partner's progress is accelerated through connecting with a spiritual group, a teacher, or waking up through a period of suffering. Sure enough, after a period of time, which can be anything from a few weeks to several years, the tension builds and the relationship ends due to the gap becoming unmanageable. The positive within these situations is that the separation is for the ultimate good. These people go on to evolve spiritually outside of the relationship.

Understanding Our Impact on People

As we make spiritual progress, the way we interact with people changes. Friends, work colleagues, family members and others may notice a difference in us. Those who are receptive will appreciate the difference and benefit from it. Others may feel threatened and belittled.

Until we have fully integrated whatever changes we have made in our life, we may find ourself judging others negatively. We might compare ourself positively to them or want to bring the unconsciousness to their attention in some way, such as telling them how well we are doing or advising them. Despite judgements and comparisons being spiritually unhelpful, this is the mind's way of trying to reassure us that what we are doing is the right thing. We do not need to resist such thoughts. We should just bring awareness and acceptance to them and then use the thoughts as a reminder that we still have some way to go before we have fully integrated the changes.

There is a responsibility to others that comes with being Present as we have the capability to bring awareness to their faults. Our Presence can even help them to confess or apologize out loud or look inwards and make positive changes. In some ways, we may know the person we are observing better than they know themselves. The faults in ourself and others are known through Presence and do not need to be analysed with conscious thought. We experience something similar when we are with others who are more Present than us. Just being in their presence allows us to see areas that we need to work on without even discussing them.

We have a choice about how we respond to faults in others. Right action might be to do something, think something, say something or simply bring acceptance to that person with no further action. Every situation is different and when we add the complexity of people into the equation, we come to realize that thought alone will not always deduce the right action. In fact, it will often trigger harmful actions. When we are lost in thought after observing somebody's faults, we react through habit, which may be inappropriate to that situation or person. When we respond through Presence, we are accessing a much deeper source of intelligence that takes everything into account before responding creatively with what is appropriate at the time. What is appropriate at the time is always what is appropriate to support the evolution of consciousness as a universal whole, which may or may not help that specific person directly. We do not need to have evidence that we have helped everybody we come into contact with to prove we are Present. Presence honours whilst transcending situations and people. It takes a much wider view on right action. The intelligence accessible through Presence can be trusted and will always be grounded in love for the whole, regardless of whether we can rationalize it with our thoughts.

POINTS FOR REFLECTION

- In absolute terms, the truth about any person is that they do not exist.

- Be receptive to those who are spiritually evolved.

- Skilful actions we take now will influence us positively in the future.

- Everything else being equal, the more Present we become, the more likely it is that we are going to connect with people who are less Present than us.

- It is sometimes necessary to remove ourself from the company of others or reduce the amount of time we spend with them.

- Decisions to create space or let go of relationships need careful consideration.

- Gaps created as we let go of old dysfunctional friendships may take a little time to fill with new conducive friendships, if indeed they need filling at all.

- When we encounter a person we find to be difficult, it is helpful to separate out the facts from our opinions and beliefs about them.

- We can love people who have attributes that we dislike and we love them by seeing beyond our ego and theirs.

- Acceptance is an internal process, which takes place within the person who is doing the accepting. They must accept their own personal experience in relation to others.

- However we are judged, if we are Present, we will respond appropriately.

- Love is the space in-between everybody and everything that enables the connection between them.

- If we are finding a person difficult, there will always be a lack of acceptance and some form of attachment on our behalf.

- We must establish a principle to focus on our own unskilfulness rather than on the unskilfulness of others.

- True communication is Presence in one person connecting with Presence in another.

- Spiritual friendship is manifested when people are Present through true communication.

- True listening is to listen to another person whilst being Present.

- Assuming people are fixed and labelling them as such does not work as it is based on an incorrect understanding of how things are.

- The more that we can understand the truth that we are part of a universal process of conditions and that the true essence of us is connected with everybody and everything else, the less we feel lonely.

- True friendship is friendship which actively supports the cultivation of Presence. False friendship actively hinders the cultivation of Presence.

- True friends can unknowingly trigger emotional pain in one another, whilst being available, understanding, supportive and Present. This leads to healing.

- Activities within true friendship are relatively unimportant as long as they are not causing harm, as the primary benefit is spiritual progress.

- Positive intentions and wishes which are based on love are a symbol of Presence, an alignment with what is, and what needs to be.

- The power is not really in our intentions, but in the wisdom that informs them and the wisdom is informed through seeing clearly.

- A spiritual relationship provides many of the benefits that come with a romantic personal relationship with the additional benefit of helping both parties to become more Present.

- It is common that one person within a relationship outgrows the other spiritually. In fact, it is inevitable as no two people are in exactly the same place and evolve at the same rate.

- Our true self accepts everyone as they are now and everything as it is now.

- We do not need to have evidence that we have helped everybody we come into contact with to prove we are Present.

- The intelligence accessible through Presence can be trusted and will always be grounded in love for the whole, regardless of whether we can rationalize it with our thoughts.

OPTIONAL LEARNING ACTIVITIES

- Recall the last time you experienced true friendship and false friendship.

- Reflect on your relationships. Do you need to make changes to who you spend time with, the activities you do together and how long you spend in one another's company?

- Bring to mind a person you find difficult and identify what it is you are attached to that is creating your inner resistance. Understand what you are expecting from them, which they are not providing, and explore how it is possible to bring acceptance to how they are now through being Present.

- When you are with people you find difficult, become more alert and intensify your awareness.

- Practise true listening with others by remaining Present through staying anchored to the breath or sensations within the body.

- Experiment with adjusting the balance between time with others and solitude. Observe how this influences your ability to remain Present.

Chapter Four

Meditation

My personal definition of meditation is "training the mind to achieve higher levels of consciousness". When we are meditating we are doing something and also doing nothing. It is about letting go and surrendering to our experience rather than distorting it. Within meditation, we are being rather than doing, and allowing positive states of mind to flourish naturally.

Meditation is a popular tool used by people to train their minds to become more aware, accepting, concentrated and Present. Meditation practice can be planned or spontaneous. By planned meditation, I am referring to consciously setting up the conditions including a place, time and technique. An example of this would be meditating whilst sitting on a cushion or chair in a peaceful spot at a given time. By spontaneous, I am referring to meditation that can take place at any time, in any place without making prior arrangements. An example of spontaneous meditation is looking at a simple object such as a table and giving it your full attention without labelling it in any way.

Planned meditation is not essential to make spiritual progress, but for many people, it is a great help. Given that meditation has benefited millions of people over thousands of years, it is well worth considering whether we should integrate it into our practice. Learning to meditate is a big challenge for most of us as it opposes what the egoic mind would prefer to do, which is to get lost in thought and create stories. Our conditions must be right in order to establish a regular and planned meditation practice, something we will be exploring in this chapter.

Time, Duration & Frequency

We must find our own balance when it comes to meditation. For some people, that balance is no meditation whilst others may spend a substantial part of their lives meditating. Many people choose a regular meditation practice of between five to sixty minutes each day. It is helpful to adjust our practice as circumstances change, and remember that every moment outside of planned meditation also provides an opportunity to cultivate mindfulness and Presence.

One of the key benefits of meditation is the clarity it provides. Generally speaking, the clearer we see things, the less we suffer. Suffering is created from an intellectual or emotional misunderstanding of how the universe really is, leading to misalignment and resistance with the present moment. Many people find that the clarity enabled through meditation leads to more energy, happiness, concentration and effectiveness in daily activities.

Occasionally I reflect on my meditation practice, but I never analyse it too much and tend to follow my intuition regarding changes. I meditate most days and I'm okay if other priorities mean I skip a day here and there. The days when I do not meditate provide reassurance that I can manage just fine without it. I also enjoy finding ways that I can integrate spontaneous meditations into the gaps between my various activities, which typically range from thirty seconds to fifteen minutes.

The conditions leading up to meditation and the time of day we meditate influence its quality and our ability to stay Present. Our energy levels fluctuate during the day so it is a good idea to select a time of day when we are usually alert. My mind is generally sharper in the mornings so I meditate then. Certain activities make our body tired and more prone to drifting off during meditation. For example, I find it difficult to stay alert after eating a substantial meal or partaking in outdoor exercise. By staying aware and reflecting on how meditation progresses, we can understand what activities help and hinder us leading up to meditation and take this into account when we plan our day and choose a time to practise. Getting the conditions and timing right for meditation is as challenging as the practice itself.

Occasionally, it is beneficial to meditate when we are feeling tired. Remember that the work we are doing in planned meditation is preparing us to be Present in our day-to-day activities. It is likely that we will experience tiredness at times when we do not have the opportunity to rest or sleep. So learning how to work with tiredness and continue to be Present until it passes is all part of the training. If my conditions do not allow me to meditate in the morning, I will meditate later on in the day. If I meditate of an evening, it is more challenging for me to stay alert. My mind is more inclined to wander off into a dream-like state. I observe this and then make an extra effort to bring myself back to the present moment by anchoring to the breath. I have learned to observe dreams for a short period of time whilst being aware of the fact I am dreaming. Being Present means being alert and relaxed simultaneously. A moderate amount of alertness is sufficient unless there is a good reason to amplify it under challenging circumstances. We can play with this balance of alertness and relaxation in our meditation and observe how it influences our practice.

Meditation Posture

A good posture is helpful for the body and especially useful when it comes to sitting meditation. We may build up our meditation practice and spend long periods of time sitting. As well as supporting and strengthening our body, a good posture allows us to cultivate a quieter mind. The mind and body are closely related. If we are experiencing bodily discomfort during meditation, there is a risk that we resist it, which leads to us being lost in thought. Meditation is about being aware of our experience and also accepting it. The intention within meditation is to keep the mind still, relaxed and alert. To help the mind enter this state, we invoke the same qualities within our bodies.

It is possible to lie flat on your back and meditate. I am yet to meet somebody that has maintained a regular and effective practice using this method, as the tendency for many is for the mind to drift off, or to fall asleep. Personally, I choose to integrate an occasional meditation whilst lying in bed. I do this once every few weeks and start the meditation session a few minutes after waking in the morning. I am more alert at that time so there is less chance of the mind drifting off. This has helped cultivate a habit of doing the same in the moments before I sleep and immediately after I wake up. I find falling to sleep and waking up with meditation to be most enjoyable. It sets me up well for a good night's sleep and greater awareness during the day.

For our planned sitting meditation, the first decision to be made is where to sit. For example, we can use a chair or sit on a meditation cushion. Wherever we sit, it must be possible to be still, relaxed and alert. If our body allows us, we should maintain a straight back and relax our shoulders. If we opt for a chair, we should select one that helps to maintain an upright-seated position rather than a chair that encourages us to slouch. If we try and meditate in a chair that is too relaxing, we may drift in and out of a dream-like state or fall asleep. Our body needs to be at right angles when seated on a chair. We observe a right angle between our torso and thighs and another right angle between our thighs and calves. Our feet should be planted firmly on the ground and the bottom of our back pushed against the back of the chair for support. We may need to bring the top of our back forward slightly on some chairs in order to establish the right angle and a straight back. This adjustment requires a small amount of work from the abdominals, back and legs to maintain an upright position, which helps keep the mind alert. We can place our hands on our lap or adopt a mudra of our choice. A mudra is a hand gesture that may symbolize an intention, such as concentration or awareness. We can use our own mudra or select one from a religion. We should ensure that our hands and arms are comfortable and promote the balance between relaxation and alertness. Our head should be evenly balanced during meditation and point straight ahead and slightly down.

We must try our best to stay very still during meditation. A still body cultivates a still mind. If we feel discomfort in our posture, such as an ache or pain, we may want to stay with it without moving for a few seconds or minutes as it will often pass without any adjustment. If we do need to move our bodies, we do so mindfully and then return to physical stillness. It helps to become comfortable and get any fidgeting out of the way before we begin.

Meditation is easier if the body is prepared beforehand by having enough sleep, exercise and eating a balanced diet. We must be prepared to have our meditation interrupted by digestion if we eat shortly before sitting. It is helpful to visit the toilet ahead of meditation and make any adjustments with our clothing to ensure we are comfortable. It is inevitable that our bodies may interrupt us in various ways during the meditation. If this happens, we simply acknowledge the interruption whatever it may be and then turn our attention back to the meditation technique we are practising.

Location, Entrance & Exit

When selecting a location for meditation, we should consider noise, aesthetics and temperature. Ideally, an area of planned meditation should be free or nearly free from noise. Background noise can be a distraction and trigger feelings and thoughts. It is helpful to have some occasional background noise and to integrate that into our meditation. The awareness and acceptance we cultivate needs to be applied outside of planned meditation where we find millions of distractions. So the odd distraction here and there as we sit can be used as a training to bring awareness to accompanying feelings and thoughts. We can then let go and regain concentration. Personally, it has been difficult for me to find silent locations in which to meditate over the years. I have often experienced noise from neighbours and household appliances. Even meditation retreat centres can be noisy due to activity around the centre's location or from sounds that others are making when meditating within a group. I have used earplugs for many years during meditation and they have done a great job keeping the distractions to a minimum. Keep in mind, that for most of us, the main distractions we experience are internal in the form of our own thoughts. Thoughts represent far more of a challenge in meditation than the odd external distraction such as some temporary noise from our environment.

The aesthetics of the meditation area influences our experience. It can help to keep the environment clean and furnish it with objects of beauty that we have a straightforward relationship with. We should not furnish the environment with objects that promote craving, as these can be distracting. A vase of flowers may be a better choice than a picture of our favourite food or somebody we find sexually attractive. We can use pictures of people or places that inspire us. The colours on display in the area may also influence our state of mind so we may want to select colours that we find more calming.

An office I worked in provided a relaxation and prayer room, which was ideal for meditating. I would go into the office early and meditate before starting work, which became an established routine. I recall occasions where I would come out of the relaxation room at work after meditating and enter straight into discussions with colleagues. On a few occasions this caused problems. People would tune in to the fact that I was in a heightened state of awareness and sensitivity which was different to my normal state and found it difficult to communicate with me as a result. They would ask me a work-related question or want to discuss issues. I would often look at them, smiling for a few seconds in silence, and I had no motivation to think about a response. We should allow space to come out of meditation before interacting with people, as we can be sensitive dependent upon how deep we go during the sit. After meditation we can sit quietly for a while or do something simple such as stretching or looking around. If we switched our phone into airplane mode during meditation, we should resist the urge to bring it back online and start using it immediately. It can help to take a few minutes after meditating to acclimatize before resuming our regular activities.

How we enter meditation is of equal importance to how we exit. We should avoid going straight into meditation after a stressful activity. It can help to sit quietly or perform some simple activities that will encourage the mind to become quieter before starting. Sitting and having a cup of tea (ideally decaffeinated) in silence may be a good option. Another option is to do something involving movement of the body. This helps us to connect with our direct experience, meaning that we become more Present prior to the meditation. I often water my plants before or after meditation. This is a simple activity with movement and a connection to nature.

Meditating outdoors in the fresh air with natural sounds around us is beneficial if there are few distractions. The main hindrance for many outdoor locations is the possibility of overhearing and then focusing on other people's discussions rather than our meditation. Personally, I find that the odd discussion from people talking as they pass by in the distance is manageable and can be integrated, but sitting somewhere with people close by is distracting. We can select locations that are quiet and remember that we will need a seat or soft ground that provides comfort for the duration of our sit.

The external temperature influences the body's ability to remain settled and comfortable. It is unnecessary to obtain the perfect temperature, but we should avoid extreme hot or cold environments. We can play around with location and posture for meditation to find a configuration that suits us. We can make changes from time to time to keep things fresh. Over the months and years our environmental conditions and bodies will change, creating the need for us to make adjustments.

Meditation Technique

When starting out in meditation, people may shop around and sample a number of different techniques before settling on one or two to practise. Techniques vary from simple breathing practices to more complex meditations involving thought designed to deepen our understanding of spiritual truths. Techniques we find in modern books are often directly lifted from or modified versions of those formulated many years ago within religions.

On a practical level, we can select meditation techniques that cultivate areas where we have a development need. For example, we may wish to be more compassionate, friendly or concentrated. There are thousands of meditation techniques designed to cultivate these and many other qualities. What we really need to be focused on is being Present, because spiritual qualities emanate out of that. If we are Present and there is a requirement for friendliness, we will be friendly. If we are Present and there is a requirement for concentration, we will be concentrated. Whatever is appropriate and skilful naturally flows when we are Present. If we practise a meditation technique that helps us to access Presence, we can manifest all these positive qualities naturally.

Meditation requires an anchor which keeps us connected to our direct experience and grounds us in the present moment. This can be any object within or outside of us, including our breath, a candle or even a sound in the background such as the humming of a refrigerator. We can try different options before settling on a single anchor upon which to establish our meditation practice. The breath is my favourite anchor as it is always available wherever I am and whatever I am doing. The breath has been used as part of meditation practice for thousands of years. If we are unsure as to which object to use for our meditation, then we should try working with the breath. The rest of this section uses the breath as an anchor for illustrative purposes. You will need to substitute and make adjustments where necessary if you are working with another anchor.

Some people choose to keep a meditation journal. This could be paper based or electronic, including mobile device apps. Journals can be used to keep a record of how often we meditate, the technique we use, conditions leading up to the meditation and any specific experiences or concerns we have. Reviewing and updating our journal can then be used as a tool for reflection and learning. A journal can also be shared with our meditation teacher if we have one.

Presence Meditation

Over the years I have practised a number of Buddhist meditation techniques, including Mindfulness of Breathing, Loving Kindness and Anapanasati on a daily basis. Whilst learning about Eckhart Tolle's teachings, I developed a meditation technique to directly cultivate Presence. Tolle acknowledges and respects planned meditation whilst not insisting upon it for progress. He encourages people to integrate meditation into their daily lives. I already had a consistent daily meditation practice established which I had faith in, so decided to continue with that and use it as another opportunity to integrate Tolle's teachings. This led to the creation of Presence Meditation.

After trying a range of different options, I found the approach I will be describing in this chapter to be the most effective way of training myself to become Present through meditation. Being in any stage of Presence Meditation is beneficial and we can move from one stage to the next at our leisure. We should be kind to ourself as we practise and move naturally through the stages at our own pace. To begin with, this technique can be practised formally as part of planned meditation. As we gain experience, we may find ourself following the same process outside of meditation. A guided audio walkthrough of the meditation is available for download at *www.darrencockburn.com.*

Presence Meditation – Stage One – Thought

Settle into your posture and gently close your eyes to begin the first stage. Closing your eyes will remove visual stimuli and make concentration easier. The first stage involves bringing awareness to your thoughts. The reason that we start here is that our thoughts are usually active prior to the start of meditation and act as the main blocker to accessing concentration. This technique differentiates itself from many others that start with the breath as the focus point. Starting with awareness of thoughts allows us to accept them and has a natural settling effect before concentrating on another meditation object such as the breath. If we skip straight to the breath without accepting our thoughts beforehand, this may be viewed by the mind as a form of resistance, control or escape. So meet your thoughts where they are with awareness and a kind acceptance and move forward from there.

If your mind is completely still to begin with then you can move directly to Stage Two. Otherwise, take some time to observe your thoughts. What is your mind doing? Is it telling stories, showing pictures or playing movies? Observing the mind in this way naturally quietens it. Observing your thoughts is similar to watching a movie at the cinema. You can watch the movie and be curious about it whilst knowing at the same time that you are not actually in the movie, because your distance from the screen gives you perspective. You can stay in this stage, observing the mind for as long as is required to quieten it. It is important not to be driven to quieten the mind, as this will create more thought. Simply observe what the mind is doing and allow it to quieten naturally. By doing this you are being the awareness that is observing the thoughts rather than getting lost in them or adding to them. You see that your awareness, which is who you really are, is separate from your thoughts, enabling perspective and freedom.

As the mind quietens and creates larger gaps between thought, you will naturally become aware of other things, including your feelings, body and breath. Once this happens and you can become aware of three full breaths without getting lost in thought, you are ready to move on to the next stage. One full breath is an in-breath followed by an out-breath. It is fine if you stay in the first stage, bringing awareness and acceptance of your thoughts for the whole time. Starting the meditation and sticking with it for the time you had planned is primary and moving through stages is secondary.

Whilst observing your thoughts, you may notice your ego at work. Chapter Five covers the ego in detail, which will help you understand more about what it is and how it operates. A common method used by the ego to reinforce itself is to create persistent thought patterns relating to things we identify with. This takes many forms, including craving, aversion, re-living the past, worry and mental story telling. If you observe your thoughts and emotions, you will find common themes that are repeated on a regular basis. These are parts of your ego. Bringing awareness to them within and outside of meditation helps to gain perspective. Let go and return to the present moment. Any thoughts that arise from the present moment will be creative and helpful. The repetitive thought patterns created by the ego are unhelpful and not who you are. Who you are is the awareness that is observing them.

So when you do catch the ego operating, this means you have regained a connection with your true essence and can mentally label it "there is the ego". That is all that is required. The ego is not good or bad so judgements are unnecessary and unhelpful. Simply, label the ego, accept it is creating thoughts and then allow the thought patterns to pass, returning to the meditation technique.

Presence Meditation – Stage Two – Breath

Once you are aware of three full breaths, you may enter the second stage. In this stage, you direct all your attention to the breath. Examine its different characteristics, including the length, frequency, texture and sound as it constantly changes. You have the whole of the breath to work with from the point where the air enters your nostrils or mouth down into the depths of your lungs. You are not trying to control the breath in any way. Simply allow it to flow naturally and operate through the body's intelligence without any conscious intervention from the mind. Your job is to give the breath your full attention, accepting whatever forms it takes.

Once you anchor to the breath in this way, it is inevitable that your awareness is going to tune in to other objects that are presented to you, including other bodily sensations, sounds, odours, feelings and thoughts. You may also be aware of subtle lights and colours even with your eyes closed. The mind may create images, movies, sounds and discussions. Being aware of these other objects instead of getting lost in them means you are Present. From here, you have two actions to take. Accept the experience without judging it and then bring your attention back to the breath.

It is human nature to become lost in thought during meditation. You may experience a feeling that triggers a thought, which leads to a story, and before you know it you have lost touch with the present moment. This happens to people (including experienced meditators) many times during meditation. Once you realize you are lost in thought, which might be several seconds or minutes into the thought stream, you can congratulate yourself because at that point you have regained your awareness. If this continues to happen, you should return to Stage One, observing the thoughts before returning to Stage Two after holding your attention for three full breaths. Never give yourself a hard time about being lost in thought within or outside of meditation. Having a continuously peaceful and concentrated mind is the vision, which can take years or even lifetimes to achieve. You should be looking for progress, not perfection. There will be ups and downs to your practice inside and outside of meditation. If you or your friends observe general progress in your level of Presence over the last few months or years, you are heading in the right direction. The most important thing is the practice itself. Stay focused on the practice and the results will take care of themselves.

When starting out, it can help to insert a count on the out-breath or in breath. For example, breathe in, breathe out, count one, breathe in, breathe out, count two and so on up to ten and then return to one. It is fine if you lose your place. Simply return to the first count and start again. This counting technique gives the mind something very simple to do, which prevents it from wandering off elsewhere. Another option practised in some forms of traditional Buddhist meditation is to mentally label each breath "long breath" or "short breath". Again, this gives the mind a simple task and stops it wandering off.

This is the second stage of Presence Meditation. It is essentially a mindfulness practice cultivating awareness, acceptance and concentration. Through using the technique in the second stage, you will be anchored to the breath and at the same time acknowledge and let go of everything else that arises within your awareness. This second stage can be practised exclusively or you can move to the third stage at any time. There is no pressure to move to the third stage. Transition between stages can be invited and should never be forced.

Presence Meditation –
Stage Three – Exclusively Present

The third stage signifies an exclusive connection with and the deepening of Presence. There are various ways into the third stage. A technique I find helpful is to direct your attention to the space or stillness in-between and around your experience. This can be used inside and outside of planned meditation. Direct your awareness in-between thoughts, feelings, bodily sensations, odours and sounds by letting them pass through your awareness. If you examine your experience closely enough, you will observe gaps and space within and around every form object that enters your awareness. This is analogous to clouds coming and going against a backdrop of the sky. You become aware and acknowledge the clouds as they pass and then return your attention to the sky. A natural consequence of this practice is that you will start to notice fewer clouds and more sky.

Connecting with the space in-between all these form objects uncovers emptiness, which is not empty. It is empty because there is no form there, just space, and at the same time it is knowable implying it is not empty. This paradox of emptiness and non-emptiness coexisting can also be described as nothing and something coexisting. If you are aware of this paradox, you are aware of the true essence that manifests all form.

This essence creates and contains your form-based identity along with everybody and everything else, which is why it feels so expansive and transcendental. You may still be aware of the breath and other experiences at this point but will no longer be focused on them as meditation objects. Instead, you will be the Presence for the experiences to manifest and play within.

The emptiness you find through looking within and around form is your awareness and connecting with this allows you to become Present. By form, I am referring to bodily sensations, things coming in through the senses, feelings and thoughts. You move away from being associated with thoughts and become the awareness or emptiness that holds and observes them. Awareness and emptiness are one and the same. When connected with emptiness, you are aware of your own awareness. When you are aware of your own awareness, you are connected with emptiness.

This awareness or emptiness does not belong to you as everybody and everything shares it. Everybody and everything in the world of form need the emptiness to exist. The emptiness, which is universal and infinite, is the creator, container and connector for all form objects at every level. Physical objects, thoughts, feelings and bodily sensations all coexist within it.

Using the method described above is helpful for those who are at the early stages in their practice as it is methodological. Another method is to bring awareness to your own awareness, if this is accessible to you. This option provides more direct access to those who are more experienced in becoming Present. Both methods lead you to the same place.

The third stage cannot be accessed through force and manifests naturally through surrendering fully to the present moment. Inviting yourself to become exclusively Present may also take you there. What you connect with in the third stage cannot be described using language. It can only be known. Words that I find helpful to point towards it are Presence, stillness, spaciousness, peace, awareness, love, the unconditioned, formlessness and emptiness. You may choose to use different words.

I find this third stage of meditation a beautiful and pleasurable experience. When you have become exclusively Present, you are aware of the fact that you are connected with something far more expansive than your limited ego-based self. Actually, the real truth is that you are not connected to it, because you are it. You cannot be connected to something that you already are. You cannot be connected to your awareness when you are your awareness. It may feel as though you are connected to something new when in fact it has been there all along but was covered up with a vale of thought. The essence of you does not fit into the usual categories that are included in mindfulness practice, such as bodily sensations, form entering through the senses, feelings or thoughts. This is what you experience, but it is not you. What you connect with in the third stage, is a very different realm to your usual form-based existence as it is formless.

I cannot offer a guaranteed technique that you can use to enter the third stage in the same way that I cannot explain how to become Present outside of planned meditation. I have offered some suggestions and in the end it is something you must know for yourself. Different people use different methods at different times to become exclusively Present. Paradoxically, the method that we use to become Present is manifested through Presence. Therefore, presence is enabling a connection with itself.

You can dwell in the third stage of Presence Meditation for any length of time from one second to several minutes. Once you are in the third stage, if you remain there and surrender to it, you can deepen your experience infinitely. At first, despite its pureness and beauty, it can be difficult to remain in the third stage. The ego has no place in the third stage and will do its best to pull you back into thoughts and stories that reinforce your false sense of self. In fact, the ego is so afraid and threatened of you being Present and radiating your true essence that it will generate feelings of fear to pull you back into thought. This explains why some people feel they are afraid of the third stage and exit meditation feeling very sensitive. It is not the people who are afraid, but their egos. There is also no concept of time in the third stage. Being exclusively Present is out of time and provides freedom from time.

During meditation, you may traverse all three stages in both directions as shown in the illustration below. You may mentally label the stage you are in for stages one and two. Stage three cannot be mentally labelled, as there will be no conscious thought. At any given time, you will either be lost in thought (which we can label Stage 0), Stage One (observing thought), Stage Two (anchored to an object such as the breath) or Stage Three (exclusively Present).

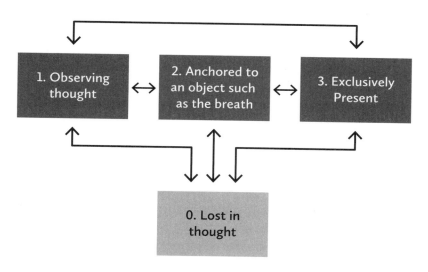

The Stages of Presence Meditation

Meditation Challenges

Meditation challenges originate from various sources, including technique. It is beneficial to select a technique and then stick with it for a while to make real progress and experience depth. Shopping around and trying a few different options is fine and we can deepen our practice later once we settle on one or two techniques. Trial and error will eventually inform us as to whether a particular technique is helpful and suitable for us at that point in time. Some people may be better suited towards meditation that involves movement, such as walking meditation, which can be planned or spontaneous. Quality texts that focus purely on meditation will highlight which techniques are suitable for beginners and advanced practitioners. If we have access to an experienced meditation teacher, they can help us select a technique. Meditation teachers are discussed later in this chapter.

As with all things, meditation can become a source of suffering if the mind is relating to it in a dysfunctional way. A common example of this is when we judge ourself. We have expectations about how our meditation should be going and if our experience does not meet our expectations, we label ourself as bad or wrong. We may compare ourself with others positively or negatively, which also creates suffering. Ego-based comparisons are futile as they work on the premise that the subject and object are both fixed and separate from each other, which is not the case. We are all part of the same expansive process that is evolving within a space that is shared. Our meditation practice is largely about acceptance. Accepting whatever experience comes up for us. People often say, "be kind to yourself" or "love yourself". How do we show kindness or love to ourself or another person? Love is present and pure when we are seeing clearly, which means working towards a full acceptance that there is, in absolute terms, no fixed form identities for us to judge.

If we are looking to establish a regular meditation practice, we can make a pledge covering the amount of meditation we plan to complete each week. We may share our commitment with friends to create some accountability. It is inevitable at some stage we will miss a meditation session we had planned. If this happens, we should bring a friendly curiosity to the situation and understand the causes. It may have been the right thing to give priority to something else that came up on the day. Maybe we had forgotten or consciously decided to do something else instead that was easier, but less helpful. Whatever the reason, if we have made a pledge, we owe it to ourself to at least understand the conditions that led to us skipping the meditation and to see if there is anything that can be done differently next time to enable it to take place. If we regularly miss our planned meditation, then something more fundamental may need to change, including the frequency, time of day or technique. If we find that our meditation targets are feeling too stretching, we can try establishing a more realistic goal by lessening the duration or frequency. If we connect well with meditation, our faith in it and motivation to practise will naturally increase over time. Remember, that there are many ways of cultivating Presence outside of planned meditation. Certain people at certain times are better suited to finding different ways to practise and this is absolutely fine.

Staying Present and preventing ourself from becoming lost in thought is our biggest challenge during meditation and life in general. Alertness and relaxation are required simultaneously to stay Present. Once our state of alertness reaches its maximum level of useful intensity, anything above that causes stress and excessive thought. Once our level of relaxation reaches a certain depth, we will fall into drowsiness, which will lead to us becoming lost in thought and experiencing a dream-like trance. Neither of these extremes is helpful within or outside of meditation. We should aim to keep ourself within the 'Presence Zone' as shown in the diagram below:

The 'Presence Zone'

Outside of meditation, we can be cultivating the right conditions for our body. We can be eating well, exercising, minimising or removing stimulants such as caffeine and alcohol and getting enough sleep. Our conditions will influence our ability to stay alert and relaxed. Working towards a simpler and more peaceful life is highly beneficial and this is discussed further within Chapter Six. Within meditation, tactics may be used to avoid anxiety and drowsiness. Temporarily controlling the breath through deepening and slowing it down can help us become more relaxed. Mentally recalling a place that we have found relaxing in the past or recalling a time when we were relaxed may also help. Taking a quick, deep in-breath can help us to become more alert. If we find ourself drifting off into a dream-like state, we may temporarily open our eyes for a few seconds or minutes. Tactics such as these are helpful props which can be used for a while and then released as we become more experienced. We should intervene as early as possible if we catch ourself drifting into an anxious or drowsy state. The earlier we intervene, the easier it will be to make any corrections and get back into the Presence Zone.

Old memories and emotions may surface during meditation. I often get flashbacks from the past during meditation. Sometimes they are from long ago when I was a small child. It can be anything from an image of the table I used to sit at during school to a memory of somebody that I knew decades ago and cannot recall consciously thinking about since. For me it is usually a still image or movie playing in my mind that is accompanied by feelings I experienced at the time. Most of the time I am lucid and aware that I am experiencing these memories. Occasionally my mind will create a dream for a few seconds or minutes before returning back to the present moment. My meditation has often extracted repressed, difficult feelings and memories from the past. It feels like a safe place where they can be held lovingly within Presence to enable healing.

Reflection & Planning

There are differences between meditation, reflection and planning. Meditation has no requirement for the realm of time whilst reflection and planning need to consider time as they are examining the past and considering the future. To function effectively in this world, reflection and planning are essential. Reflection enables us to learn from our experience and planning enables us to get our basic needs met and achieve goals. Even the practice of cultivating Presence benefits from reflection and planning. We can reflect upon the times when we were lost in thought, understand the preceding conditions and then plan for changes in the future to help ourself. Conversely, we can reflect and learn from periods of time when our state of Presence was more sustained or deeper than usual.

Time can be allocated to reflection and planning, leading to an increased learning from the past and wise decisions about the future. There are various techniques you can refer to that cover these two areas in depth so I shall not go into them in detail here. The amount of time you need to allocate will be dependent upon the complexity of your life. You can start with as little as five minutes if you have a busy schedule, see how that works out and increase the time later. If you do not reflect and plan consciously, your mind will grab opportunities to do so when there is a space available, such as when you sit down to meditate. Operating systems running inside computers function in the same way. They have certain maintenance tasks they need to carry out which they perform when the computer is not fully utilized.

When we meditate without creating opportunities to reflect and plan, the space allocated to meditation will always be at risk of being taken by reflection or planning. This can lead to frustration as we have an expectation to meditate and be Present which is not being met. This type of reflection and planning is reactive and may be triggered by the ego in response to hindrances such as worry or anxiety. The quality of any decisions or conclusions from ego-led reflection or planning is low. Reflection and planning, which are triggered by the ego are a reaction to fear and an attempt to control things to help keep our false sense of identity safe. When thoughts or action are rooted in fear, the quality of anything manifesting from them is low.

If we do become aware of reflection or planning during meditation, there are three antidotes we can apply. The first is to plan time for reflection and planning. The second is to work towards making our life simpler. The less complex our life, the less reflection is required to review the past and the less planning is required to influence the future. The third and most powerful antidote is to become more Present. One of the main reasons we have to reflect is due to the problems or dramas we have created about the past or future whilst being lost in thought. Becoming more Present makes planning for the future simpler as we can access a source of wisdom and creativity that flows through our thinking, which increases the quality of our decisions.

It is quite normal in meditation or at other times for our untrained minds to drift off into the past and future. We have to consciously train our minds to keep coming back to the present moment. The more we do this, the easier it becomes. Planned meditation is a great opportunity for this training and there are so many other opportunities available to us. Bringing awareness to bodily sensations whilst drifting off to sleep is one example. Another example is becoming aware of other cars and the road conditions whilst driving. In fact, any time when we are prone to becoming lost in thought is an opportunity to train the mind to stay Present.

Being lost in thought during meditation, regardless of the theme, may be a response to our mind using thought to escape from unpleasant feelings. It is a good idea to tune in to our bodies and understand if there are unpleasant feelings present. If there are, the only action required during meditation is to give them our full attention. We let go of any thoughts or story telling that the mind creates to use an escape route. We go into the body and face the feelings fully, which is the only way to release the underlying emotional pain. Most unpleasant feelings pass within a couple of minutes if we give them our full attention, which is what they need. We may need to do this several times before the underlying pain is released altogether. Through releasing unpleasant feelings and thoughts we are healing and purifying ourself and gaining access to the peace and wisdom that is inherent within Presence. We are also reducing the need for our addictive patterns that are used as an escape route from the pain.

I have experienced meditation practice drifting into unconscious reflection and planning on a regular basis. It tends to happen more during challenging times or times of greater complexity in my life. If we let unconscious reflection and planning happen during meditation, it can easily become an ingrained habit which our minds then default to when we attempt to meditate.

We should remind ourself of the technique we will be following during meditation and set an intention to follow that technique diligently before we close our eyes to begin. This can be enough to wake us up from the habit of using meditation as an opportunity to reflect or plan and focus us on staying Present. Meditating with others, guided meditation and working with a meditation teacher are other options for keeping our meditation practice fresh and focused.

Teachers, Groups & Religious Movements

Some people find it helpful to have a meditation teacher guide them. A meditation teacher can help with technique and be available to answer any questions we may have. We may have times when we are not motivated to meditate, experience frustration due to a perceived lack of progress or become ambitious about achieving certain goals or states of consciousness. A good meditation teacher helps to ground us, bring us back into the present moment and help us to accept whatever we are experiencing in a non-judgemental way.

We should make our choice of teacher wisely before allowing ourself to be guided by them. Teachers and religious movements may provide you with access to meditation retreats. You can learn more about teachers, retreats and religious movements in Chapter Eleven. Keep in mind that a religious movement offering meditation guidance may be analogous to a river with a strong undercurrent that draws you in. Metaphorically speaking, if it is beneficial to you to flow in the direction of the river, then you can choose to allow the current to take you. If you are unsure, then you always have the option of getting out and watching the river flow from the bank. You can sit on the bank for a while, move away from the bank, jump back in or swim in another river.

Involvement with any religious movement is only sustainable and beneficial if it supports a connection with who you really are. Not your false sense of self, but who you are in your essence.

Mini Meditations

There are countless opportunities to meditate for a short period of time throughout the day. Each time we meditate, even if only for a few seconds, we are re-establishing our connection with Presence. Punctuating our day with mini meditations keeps us grounded and reduces the risk of becoming lost in thought. We can experiment with different techniques and select a few that work for us.

Here are a few options I have used myself. Each option can be practised from a few seconds to a few minutes:

- **Focus on the aliveness and energy within the hands or anywhere else within the body.** If you find this difficult, you can position your hands so that the palms are facing upward and visible. If you pay close attention, you will feel a tingling within the hands and the fingertips may be sensitive. If you cannot feel this energy, then try zooming your attention into different fingers or the palms. You may also move the fingers and hands very slightly to help experience the aliveness within them.

- **Take a number of conscious breaths.** Control the breath by making it a little slower and deeper. Whilst doing this, pay attention to the different characteristics of the breath in the same way that is advised in Presence Meditation. Examine its texture, length, sound, speed, depth and the different areas of the body that it traverses. This is a particularly useful technique if you are feeling anxious, as the depth and slowness of the breath will help you relax.

- **Have a stretch whilst sitting, standing or lying down.** Interlock your fingers and stretch your hands and arms high above your head. As you do this, feel all the sensations in the body. If this induces a long out-breath or yawn, then experience this consciously. After the stretch, relax the body and bring your awareness to the parts of the body that you were aware of during the stretch including the fingers, arms and shoulders.

- **Take your awareness into the body and hunt for feelings.** You can ask yourself "How am I feeling now?" There is a whole range of pleasant and unpleasant feelings you might be experiencing, including anxiety, arousal, stress, sadness, happiness, tiredness, fear or peace. You may also be feeling neutral and unable to identify any pleasant or unpleasant feelings, which is fine. No commentary or judgements are required with this technique. Mentally label any feeling you find with a word or two and then expand your awareness back out to the rest of your body.

- **Place your attention onto an object.** Ideally something natural, which could be a tree, the sky or a bird. Simultaneously bring awareness to your breath. By placing your attention on an object and your breath, your mind will leave little opportunity to think, helping you to meditate and be Present.

Mini meditations can be interspersed throughout your daily activities spontaneously. They can also be trained to become habitual when undertaking certain activities. For example, you may complete a mini meditation:

- When you sit in a car before the engine starts. Similarly, once the car is stationary before you open the door to exit.
- Whilst seated on a bus, train or other form of public transport.
- Standing in a queue.
- Before and after a meal.
- After completing an activity on your computer or phone.
- Whilst you are taking a walk (if safe to do so).
- In-between reading the pages of a book.
- Whilst lying in bed before going to sleep of an evening or getting up in the morning.

If you enjoy using technology and gadgets, you may choose to take the opportunity to integrate them into your planned meditation. There is a wide range of mobile applications available to support meditation including timers and guided meditations. Thousands of guided meditations can be found on teachers' websites and YouTube. Be careful, though, as it is easy to get lost in all the options and continuously hunt for a better application or teacher. Keep this in mind and once you find an application or guided meditation that works for you, stick with it for a while.

Motivation

We should examine and reflect upon our motives for meditation, checking to see that it is beneficial to our well-being and spiritual progress. Positive reasons for meditating include using it as a training to cultivate mindfulness, concentration, loving kindness and Presence. We may also be motivated by how peaceful or enjoyable meditation feels as it provides us with a mechanism to have a break from the usual thoughts and activities in daily life.

Meditation can be used as a false refuge to avoid other activities or situations that need our attention. Whether we are conscious of it or not, we have the wisdom within us to know what we need to be doing. If we are meditating when we really need to be doing something else, the practice will be uncomfortable and difficult due to the tension created. Ideally, we should partake in activities that we are motivated towards rather than using them as an escape from something else we really need to be doing. Even within the context of all the positive benefits, meditation can become an addiction and used as an escape from facing and working through emotional pain, difficult situations or activities. If we do not consciously intervene, the prioritization may self-regulate. The tension created through using meditation as an escape activity may eventually become too great and the meditator will then face his or her challenges.

If we plan to meditate and find that our mind is producing lame excuses for why we should avoid it, then we should let go of the excuses and meditate anyway. The ego is threatened by meditation because it helps to diminish it. This is the same for any practice that cultivates Presence. The ego kicks and screams by providing reasons and excuses for not completing helpful practices as a reaction to feeling threatened. We can lean on our intuition here and sense when this is the case, as the excuses that our mind creates will not feel credible. That said, there are times when we should not meditate and in these instances we feel much more integrated around a decision to skip a session for the right reasons. Needing sleep or relaxation are both valid reasons for not meditating. If we are genuinely tired, then it is best to rest or sleep. If our minds are wired from a busy day, it may help to relax first and unwind before meditating. The challenge here is to ensure that we get enough sleep and relaxation, which supports our meditation practice and levels of Presence, in general. The quality of our meditation provides a useful feedback mechanism against the general balance we are maintaining.

We must be mindful of our egos when it comes to meditation. The ego can view meditation as some kind of competition and draw comparisons with others. I have experienced this a lot in the past. A key motive for meditating so much and attending lots of meditation retreats was to help myself feel as though I was more evolved than others. My ego used it as a prop to artificially boost my self-esteem and it was accompanied by a judgmental attitude towards others and myself. This unskilful and harmful motive caused a great deal of stress. I also recall meditating in public places deliberately in order to draw attention to myself, which is the ego again, but in a different guise. There are no specific interventions I can recommend in these situations other than to bring awareness to how the ego is operating if possible, which is a meditation in itself. Right action will flow naturally from there.

Presence Meditation – Quick Reference Guide

STAGE ONE – Thought

1. Settle into your posture and gently close your eyes.

2. If your mind is already quiet and peaceful, move directly to Stage Two.

3. If your mind contains thoughts, observe the mind – be the observer.

4. Acknowledge whether your mind is creating words, stories, pictures or movies.

5. If you recognize the ego, label it mentally, "that is the ego".

6. Do not judge the ego or anything else that enters your awareness. Simply accept the experience and allow it to pass.

7. As you observe your mind, invite it to become quieter.

8. As the mind quietens, become aware of other objects that enter your awareness, including feelings, breath, bodily sensations and things coming in through the senses.

9. Allow yourself to become aware of three full breaths. One full breath is an in-breath followed by an out-breath.

10. Stay in this stage as long as you need to become aware of three full breaths without being lost in thought.

11. Once you are aware of three full breaths without getting lost in thought, you can move to Stage Two.

STAGE TWO – Breath

1. Direct all your attention to the breath.

2. Allow the breath to flow naturally. Do not control the breath.

3. Examine its different characteristics, including the length, frequency, texture and sound as it constantly changes.

4. Be aware of the whole of the breath from the point where the air enters your nostrils or mouth down into the depths of your lungs.

5. If you become aware of other objects, such as bodily sensations, sounds, smells, feelings and thoughts, simply acknowledge them and allow them to pass.

6. Do not judge your experience regardless of what it consists of. Accept your experience and remain anchored to the breath.

7. If you are finding it difficult to focus on the breath, insert a count after the out-breath or before the in-breath. Count to ten and then return to one. If you lose count, return to one.

8. If you become aware that you are completely lost in thought, then return to Stage One and observe your thoughts.

9. Once you are fully anchored to the breath for a period of time, you can move to Stage Three.

STAGE THREE – Exclusively Present

1. Direct your attention to the space in-between and around your experience.

2. Look in-between thoughts, feelings, bodily sensations, odours and sounds by allowing them to pass through your awareness.

3. Observe gaps and space within and around every object that enters your awareness.

4. If this is not possible at this time, then return to Stage Two.

5. Stay connected with the space and emptiness that you find, which merges with your awareness.

6. Explore the space and emptiness. Explore your awareness. Allow yourself to enjoy its stillness and serenity.

7. Retain your connection to the space and emptiness. This is Presence.

8. If you find yourself becoming lost in thought, then return to Stage One.

Exiting the Meditation

1. When your timer signifies the end of the meditation session or your meditation comes to a natural end, gently open your eyes.

2. Remain in your meditation posture for at least thirty seconds, taking in your surroundings.

3. Stay mindful as you leave your meditation area and avoid any demanding activities for a few minutes until you have acclimatized to your usual environment.

POINTS FOR REFLECTION

- Meditation is training the mind to achieve higher states of consciousness.

- Suffering is created from an intellectual or emotional misunderstanding of how the universe really is, leading to misalignment and resistance with the present moment.

- The time of day when we meditate and preceding conditions influence the quality of meditation and our ability to stay Present.

- Occasionally, it is beneficial to meditate when we are feeling tired.

- A good posture is helpful for the body and especially useful when it comes to sitting meditation.

- The intention within meditation is to keep the mind still, relaxed and alert.

- We must try our best to stay very still during meditation because a still body cultivates a still mind.

- We should be conscious of how we enter and exit meditation.

- Journals can be used to keep a record of how often we meditate, the technique we use, conditions leading up to the meditation and any specific experiences or concerns.

- Some people may be better suited towards meditation that involves movement, including walking meditation.

- Meditation can become a source of suffering if the mind is relating to it in a dysfunctional or addictive way.

- If we are looking to establish a regular meditation practice, we can make a pledge about the amount of meditation we plan to complete each week.

- We must be simultaneously alert and relaxed to stay Present.

- When we meditate without creating opportunities to reflect and plan, the space allocated to meditation will always be at risk of being taken by reflection or planning.

- We make our choice of meditation teacher wisely before allowing ourself to be guided by them.

- Each time we meditate, even if only for a few seconds, we have the opportunity to become Present.

- Punctuating our day with mini meditations keeps us grounded and reduces the risk of becoming lost in thought.

- If we plan to meditate and find that our mind is producing lame excuses for why we should avoid it, then we should let go of the excuses and meditate anyway.

- The real measure of the effectiveness of our planned meditation is how it contributes to our level of Presence outside of meditation.

- Decisions made whilst we are Present are wise decisions.

OPTIONAL LEARNING ACTIVITIES

Download the guided walkthrough for Presence meditation and try the practice each day for one week (www.darrencockburn.com).

- Locate and attend a local meditation class.

- Punctuate your days with spontaneous meditation.

- Research a range of different meditation techniques.

- Create an environment at home where you can meditate regularly.

- Try some meditation apps.

- Create a meditation schedule and stick to it.

- Keep a meditation journal and reflect on your practice.

- Create time for reflection and planning.

Chapter Five

Internal Hindrances
& The Ego

I was a practising Buddhist for many years and during that time I learned a lot about meditation from some good teachers. Buddhist teachings provide helpful lists and tips that can be applied within meditation and life in general. You could say that any activity where you are Present is a form of meditation. One list that I find particularly useful is The Five Hindrances. This will be introduced within this chapter along with the ego, which is the ultimate hindrance. The Eight Worldly Conditions that the ego feeds upon are also introduced.

The challenges we face within our meditation practice or any other activity resulting in a lack of concentration and being lost in thought will be due to one or more hindrances[6], which are (i) sensory desire (ii) ill will (iii) sloth and torpor (iv) restlessness/worry and (v) doubt. We will explore each in turn and the antidotes we can use to overcome them. The chapter has been titled *Internal* Hindrances & The Ego to reflect the fact that hindrances always come from within, but may be triggered by external factors. This is empowering as it highlights that it is within our gift to be able to apply the antidotes and set up the conditions to be free of these hindrances and be continuously Present.

Sensory Desire

Sensory desire is the first hindrance, which covers cravings we have for things entering the senses, including sight, sound, taste, smell and bodily sensations. We can crave for just about anything from the taste of a particular food, the pleasure from sex or a beautiful view in a location we enjoy. The ego is never satisfied with our experience of sensory pleasure. It uses attachment to previous pleasures and greed[7] for more pleasure as a way of feeding and strengthening itself.

An antidote to sensory desire is examination through giving the craving your full attention. Become fully aware of the experience and understand what it consists of. What exactly is your experience? Are there associated bodily sensations? How does the craving make you feel? What are you thinking at the time? When I was addicted to caffeine, I often craved for it during meditation. On examination of the craving, I found that it consisted of a slight watering of the sides of my mouth followed by thoughts about preparing a coffee. I observed all this within the meditation. When we look at things in this way, we observe patterns and processes taking place within us, which provides space and perspective between the craving and us. We can shift from being lost thinking about the craving to being the consciousness that is aware of it. This helps to break down cravings and remove our identifications with them.

The positive opposite to sensory desire is contentment. A positive consequence of becoming more Present is that we naturally make a transition from sensory desire towards seeking contentment. The mind becomes more peaceful, and we come to respect and enjoy that peace far more than desperately trying to fill our life with sensory pleasure.

If we are content during our meditation or any other activity we will be free from craving. Contentment comes about through setting up the right conditions in our life, ensuring that our basic needs are met and cultivating Presence. If we are regularly experiencing a particular craving during meditation it may be that we need to understand the craving more by exploring it outside of meditation. Often, the simple process of bringing awareness to our cravings and understanding what they consist of can be enough to break them down and allow them to pass. Some cravings are quite natural and created in response to our human needs. We may crave for sex during meditation, which could cause our mind to create images, start a chain of thought about how or when we will get it, trigger feelings or bodily sensations. We might crave for food if we are hungry. Our human nature triggers many cravings. All that is required is to observe our experience and let the craving pass without adding anything like judgements or extensions to what the mind or body has already manifested.

A craving can be natural or unnatural. We may crave for food because we are hungry, which is perfectly natural or we may crave for food to escape from emotional pain, which is unnatural. If the craving originates from a state of Presence then it will be natural. All unnatural craving originates from being lost in thought. Presence allows natural cravings like hunger and sleep, which represent our basic needs to be seen clearly. We can use our awareness and reflect on our experience to discern each craving type. It is fine to enjoy life's pleasures so long as we are not harming ourself or others in the process. If we are Present when faced with the option of partaking in harmful pleasures, we will forgo the pleasure. We are guided to do the right thing by a force that transcends our ego's selfish cravings.

When it comes to sensory pleasures there is no need to go hunting for them when we are Present. We simply stay aware and allow them to find us. Simple pleasures are everywhere when we are receptive to them. The formation of the clouds, birds, flowers, trees, the feeling of our breath and the beauty we recognize in people to name just a few. When we are Present, the crude unhelpful pleasures can be discarded whilst the pure, more refined pleasures can be enjoyed. We can delight in pleasure or allow it to intoxicate us. When we are Present, we delight in pleasure. When we are lost in thought, the pleasure will intoxicate us. True pleasure can only be experienced when we are Present.

Sensory pleasure is always temporary and never ultimately satisfying, which is why our minds create suffering after we have craved for it. We are craving something that can never ultimately fulfil us. When pleasure originates from a natural source and presents itself to us without craving, we can enjoy it fully as long as it is not harmful. Through our practice we may see a shift from craving sensory pleasures to more refined pleasures, such as the arts, nature and true communication with others. The reason for the shift is that refined pleasures increase our level of Presence, whereas sensory pleasures we crave for reduce it. Sensory pleasures consumed without awareness lead to intoxication, which often generates excessive thinking and a high, which is outside of our conscious field of awareness. As our field of awareness grows through our practice, we are better placed to contain the highs and the lows, holding more of what life presents to us with equanimity and skill.

Ill Will

Ill will is a hindrance that covers feelings and thoughts that are based upon wanting to harm people, which may include ourself. It also includes feelings of hatred or rejection towards situations. The ego triggers this hindrance based upon its sense of separateness. It needs to judge people or situations to reinforce or strengthen its identifications. Ill will may arise towards people we view as blockers to us achieving goals we have identified with. Also, if we are attached to the experience or outcomes we gain from others, including friends, work colleagues, our partner or family members, we may feel ill will towards anybody that appears to threaten our relationship with them. Many types of unpleasant feelings relate to ill will, including jealousy, envy, hostility, anger, resentment and bitterness. People may also experience ill will towards themselves, representing a dissonance between how they think they should be and how they are in reality. This creates feelings of self-hatred or guilt.

As referenced earlier, ill will may also be directed towards a situation rather than a specific individual. For example, if we were in resistance to a holiday that was cancelled due to some external factor such as bad weather, we may experience ill will towards the situation if there is not a specific individual or group to blame. We make judgements when we expect a situation to be different from what it actually is at that point in time, which is clearly delusional and at odds with how things are. That expectation is created by the ego in response to its belief that you and the rest of the world should align with its agenda. Seeing clearly allows us to let go of all this, leading to more peace, acceptance and love.

If we find ourself feeling angry towards a person or situation, it is worth keeping in mind that the root cause of that anger might be from the past. When we repress anger through a lack of awareness or failure to express it in the context it was generated, it is stored within us and adds to our ego. It is then possible for people and situations to trigger these old feelings, which are often irrational and inflated. I repressed a lot of anger within my childhood and had no environment where it could be expressed safely. Some anger was expressed in ways that were harmful when I was a child and the rest of it was carried into adulthood. I continued to experience the old feelings of anger in new situations where it was unnecessary and unjustified. The ego is very sneaky and will create all sorts of fantasies and stories to falsely justify anger. Being Present with unpleasant feelings helps to heal us and release them. We should accept any feelings of anger, giving them what they need, which is our full attention. We can explore the feelings within the body and return to them if the mind wanders and creates stories. Usually, within the space of a few minutes, the anger passes. If we can be Present with unpleasant feelings as they arise without adding stories, we will reduce the ego and gain freedom from them.

The positive opposite to ill will is acceptance. If we accept situations, others and ourself, we will be free from ill will. How do we bring about acceptance of people and situations? Strictly speaking, the reality is that we cannot, but we can accept the thoughts and feelings that we are having about them. Acceptance only really applies within us and within the present moment. The past has gone and the future does not exist yet. If we can accept what is now, then we are free. Ill will is only an issue when our mind is lost in the realm of time. Acceptance is explored further in Chapter Nine.

Loving kindness towards people is another antidote for ill will. This can be practised externally through kind speech or physical acts of love and generosity. Taking positive action towards a person can break down ill will and replace it with love. We have to be careful about how we do this because if we engineer acts of kindness through ego-based thought, there will be a lack of integrity in our communication. You may have experienced this before when it feels like somebody is trying too hard to be friendly or kind. It feels uncomfortable because the action comes from the other person's ego and the need to control rather than love.

True kindness and love flow spontaneously through Presence. An alternative to thinking our way to loving and kind actions when we are with people is to take up a loving kindness meditation practice such as Metta Bhavana. Metta Bhavana is a Buddhist meditation practice which cultivates loving kindness to ourself and all beings, including friends, people we have neutral feelings towards, enemies and everybody else in the world. Metta is a word that originates from the ancient Pali language and loosely translates to love. The word Bhavana originates from the same language and means 'to cultivate'. So Metta Bhavana is the cultivation of love. You can adjust this practice to take situations as well as people into account. This practice creatively cultivates loving kindness in meditation through thought. This then leads to spontaneous loving thoughts, speech and action outside of meditation when we are Present. More information on this widely practised form of meditation is available from Buddhist sources, including books from Sharon Salzberg[8], a leading author on the subject.

Our vision should be to consistently accept our experience and always respond to ourself with love. This should apply whether we are practising meditation or doing other things. We should never criticize what the mind does. We can and should take responsibility for correcting our own errors and even that must come from a place of love to be effective. I appreciate that this can be challenging when we make mistakes or notice harmful thoughts. Our ability to practise effectively is influenced by our past. If we were lucky enough to have kind and accepting adults around us when we were growing up, that would certainly help as it will have trained us to respond to ourself in the same way. The reverse is true in that we will be more challenged with this practice if we had adults around us who blamed and criticized us. Either situation is fine. The good news is that the brain is flexible enough to make it possible to create new habits and we can retrain our minds to align with the truth once we understand it. If we can be aware of negative self-judgements during or after they are made, that is a good start. We can then remind ourself that we are human beings with our own past conditioning whilst knowing that we are works in progress just like everybody else. If we reflect on these truths, we will soon become more accepting of ourself.

Sloth & Torpor

The next hindrance is sloth and torpor, which covers mental or physical tiredness compromising our state of alertness. Feelings of laziness, drowsiness, heaviness, lethargy and weariness may be present when this hindrance is active. What we experience within meditation gives us feedback on our general well-being. Tiredness during meditation often points to basic bodily issues that can be resolved through getting more sleep, exercising or correcting our diet. It can also be triggered due to emotional problems linked to frustration, boredom or hopelessness. Sloth and torpor lead to a lack of concentration within and outside of meditation manifested in a dream-like state, which takes us below thought. One of the antidotes is investigation. Mental and physical tiredness are subjective feelings or labels we use to generalize underlying feelings and experiences. If we feel tired, we can ask ourself what the tiredness is and develop a curiosity to explore it. How does the "tiredness" feel? Where in the body is it located? What are we thinking? On closer examination, we will find that there are subtle differences to every bout of tiredness. Examining the tiredness in this way may allow us to rise above it and regain alertness.

Other practical antidotes to sloth and torpor are taking a nap if the body is tired, or doing something to rouse energy, such as taking a brisk walk. There are also tactics that we can apply within a meditation session. We can try taking a deep in-breath and filling our lungs with oxygen, which boosts physical energy. Another option is to open our eyes for a few moments or imagine bright white light, which can help regain alertness. The time that we meditate makes a big difference, as our bodies will naturally vary throughout the day. We can experiment with this to determine whether certain times of the day are more conducive to being alert. The positive opposite to sloth and torpor is alertness.

Restlessness & Worry

The fourth hindrance is restlessness and worry. Restlessness can be physical due to pain or discomfort. Discomfort is a dull, moderately uncomfortable ache in one or more parts of the body whereas pain has a sharper texture and manifests suddenly. Discomfort may be accepted, but pain should always be addressed. If we are in pain during meditation, we should take a moment to mindfully make an adjustment or take steps outside of meditation to investigate. Practices such as yoga that strengthen the body and improve flexibility can help us sit more comfortably for longer periods. Physical restlessness is always temporary and we can try sitting with it for a while to see if it passes. I often experience the urge to scratch my nose or other parts of my body during meditation. If I accept the experience, remaining calm and still, it usually passes within a few seconds. The same goes for the odd ache or pain here and there. I do the same if insects land on me. I allow them to do what they need to do and be on their way.

Mental restlessness and worry can be worked on within and outside of meditation. Within meditation, we should keep the body very still and relaxed, waiting patiently. The mind will then follow. Also, focusing on a single point such as the breath naturally calms the mind. Temporarily lengthening the out-breath will have a relaxing effect, helping settle restlessness and worry. If we experience regular themes that cause us to worry, we can work on them outside of meditation. This may involve self-investigation, discussion with friends or professional support.

For years, money and work were regular themes causing me to worry and become restless during meditation. Outside of meditation and on the surface of my life, everything was fine. I had enough money and my work conditions were positive. The worry was being triggered by my subconscious mind and based upon unresolved issues I had experienced years before. The money worries were inherited from my parents and the work anxiety was due to some traumatic experiences earlier in my career. My subconscious mind was triggering various emotions in an attempt to protect me from old threats and beliefs that were no longer present or relevant. The subconscious mind was doing what it thought was helpful, but it was actually out of date. As powerful as it is, the subconscious mind causes problems by failing to take time into account and often constrains us by reacting inappropriately. An absence of understanding of the present moment is the main constraint of the subconscious mind, which causes a great deal of suffering when people are lost in thought. There is usually no real problem here and now, but the subconscious mind will take in stimulus, link it to the past, believe that old reactions from the past are relevant in the present and then react by triggering thoughts or emotions that are out of date and unhelpful. When we are lost in thought, we are open to reacting based on old patterns. When we are Present, any responses are relevant and creative based upon the needs of the moment.

When we examine the present moment, we find the majority of the time everything is just fine. Worry creates negative thoughts due to perceived threats and a fear of what the future might hold. Fear is generated by the ego due to its fixed and constraining preferences about how things should be. If we do experience feelings of worry, they should always be accepted and never resisted. Our mind is warning us about a perceived problem with the future based on what it has experienced before. It is like a friend who has good intentions by trying to help us, but is providing irrelevant and unhelpful advice. Sometimes, the fact that we are worrying may be a helpful call to action. Once we return to the present moment, we will know whether intervening actions are required and whether the worry is relevant. Presence brings an effective filtering mechanism to worry and other difficult feelings. It allows us to access wisdom, to discard irrelevant worries and action relevant worries.

Attachments and addictions become more visible to ourself or others during times of restlessness and worry. Because the mind is full of thought at these times, our connection to wisdom and creativity is lost and we fall back into old patterns. We miss the opportunity to respond skilfully and creatively to what the situation needs and resort to doing what we have done previously, which is often irrelevant and unhelpful. It is acting out of a dream-like state rather than being fully awake and responsive in the present moment.

Worry is sometimes experienced in relation to irrational guilt. We may end up worrying about something and suffering when there is no need to. I recall a time when I was having dinner with a friend who had been experiencing some pain. The doctor suspected it was due to gallstones and signed him off from work for a few days. My friend told me that he felt guilty when he was sick and absent from work. On this occasion, his reasons for being absent from work were justified. I was very Present when I was listening to him and without thinking about it, I spontaneously asked him if he had times in the past when he had taken sick leave from work or school when he was fit and well. He did not enjoy going to school or have the capacity to deal with the emotional pain it was causing him at the time. He told me he used to eat soap to cause sickness that provided an excuse to stay home, which led to him feeling guilty. This is a classic example of an addictive thought pattern being created during childhood. Because the addiction had not been released, the underlying pain was re-activated under certain circumstances. Unresolved pain from childhood will be taken into adulthood. In the case of my friend, it must have been some forty years after his issues at school. Once he faces the pain and gives it the attention it needs, he will be free of his addiction, irrational guilt and the associated worry. After he told me about this, we both laughed. We were not laughing at his pain, but at the fact that we had uncovered what was causing his irrational guilt. Sometimes, when you discover something that is truthful, it can release a burst of energy that manifests as a laugh. I often laugh when I am listening to spiritual teachers or reading books that provide 'light bulb moments' of understanding.

Take a minute or two to stop reading and examine the present moment. Not the past or future, just now. What problems do you have right now? Usually, you have no problems in the present moment. Occasionally, if you are in physical or emotional pain you might have a problem, but the rest of the time there are no problems at all. The positive opposite to restlessness and worry is what you find when you are Present, which is ease and calmness.

Doubt

The fifth and final hindrance from the list is doubt. Its scope covers self-doubt, doubt in our practice and doubt in our spiritual teachers. This includes doubt in meditation, training courses, techniques, organizations or religions we might be involved in. Doubt can hinder us from planning to meditate or meditating at the times we had planned. It is also a hindrance within meditation itself, causing the mind to create thoughts and stories about why we should not be meditating or questioning our ability. These thoughts and stories then take us below thought and away from a concentrated state. Bringing awareness to doubt and acknowledging it honestly opens up the door to a resolution and progress. The positive opposite to doubt is trust and conviction. The amount of peace and happiness we experience in our life regardless of worldly conditions is proportional to the amount of faith we have in the present moment.

At times, we may not have faith in the value of meditation or our spiritual practice, which is quite normal. If that is where we are then we must acknowledge it. Faith builds over time as we practise more and experience the benefits.

Studying quality texts on meditation, using guided meditations, working with a teacher and meditating in a group may help to build confidence and faith. If we doubt the meditation technique we are using, doubt our teacher or doubt our religion, then the antidote is to investigate and understand more about the situation. This can be done through reading, speaking to friends or speaking with our teacher if we have one. It is good to find a full resolution if possible to help prevent the doubt from returning at a later point.

Hindrances Summary

The table below provides the list of hindrances along with their antidotes and positive opposites.

Hindrance	Description	Antidote Options	Positive Opposite
Sensory Desire	Cravings we have for things entering the senses including sight, sound, taste, smells and bodily sensations	Examination through giving the craving our full attention	Contentment
Ill Will	Feelings and thoughts that are based upon wanting to harm people including wanting to harm ourself	Acceptance Loving Kindness	Acceptance / Love
Sloth & Torpor	Mental or physical tiredness compromising our state of alertness	Investigation Resting Rousing energy Deep in-breath Eyes open wide	Alertness
Restlessness & Worry	Physical restlessness Mental restlessness and worry	Adjusting body Strengthening body Still body Focusing on single point Lengthening out-breath Investigating causes for worry	Ease & Calmness
Doubt	Includes self-doubt, doubt in our spiritual practice and doubt in our spiritual teachers	Investigation and possible interventions/ changes	Trust & Conviction

Summary of Hindrances, Antidotes and Positive Opposites

Application outside of Meditation

Meditation is similar to the game of snakes and ladders where hindrances represent the snakes and their positive opposites represent the ladders. If you study the hindrances and practise working with them, they can be applied outside of meditation. Most activities can be hindered by sensuous desire, ill will, sloth and torpor, restlessness and worry, and doubt. Those same activities can be helped by the positive opposites, which are contentment, love, alertness, calmness, trust and conviction. Similarly, if we practise Presence Meditation, we can apply it to good effect in our other activities. Most people spend more of their life outside of planned meditation than within planned meditation. Therefore, it follows that most of the benefit of the guidance in this chapter can be realized in our daily activities outside of meditation.

If we train by working with the hindrances within our meditation, we will find that the quality of the rest of our life will improve as a positive consequence. One of the secrets of effective meditation is to learn to meditate outside of planned meditation in our daily activities. Planned meditation can then be viewed in the right perspective as training for life or even something that we may do because we find it pleasurable. Most of the time, I thoroughly enjoy sitting to meditate and believe it is far more beneficial than engaging in crude and harmful pleasures. The real measure of the effectiveness of our planned meditation is how it contributes to our level of Presence outside of planned meditation.

The Ego

The ego is the ultimate hindrance to being Present. I first came across the concept of the ego whilst reading Eckhart Tolle's teachings[1]. I use the word concept for a reason because there is nothing real or fixed about the ego. It is a useful label to help us understand a process and dysfunctional human phenomenon. I refer to the ego quite a few times within this book so feel it necessary to explain a little more about what it is and how it works. My understanding is that Tolle describes the ego as thought and emotional patterns that are persistently repeated due to our strong identifications with them[2]. There are a multitude of other spiritual descriptions. For example, Deepak Chopra's website[9] describes the ego as our self-image rather than our true self. There are also psychological explanations such as Sigmund Freud's positioning of the ego as a mediator within a conceptual model of mental functioning, but we do not need to go into that here. For our purposes and within the context of this book we will work with my interpretation of the description provided by Tolle.

The ego consists of mind activity that we identify with, which can be of a positive or negative nature. The mind activity can be about having something or having nothing. For example, we may identify with being a great tennis player, a poor public speaker or both. We may identify with being a mother, a daughter, a husband or a wife. We may identify with being stylish or dowdy. We may identify with being popular or unpopular. We may identify with being peaceful or angry. We may identify with an unskilful behaviour or addiction. We may identify with having a luxurious car or having no car. All of these examples may be identifications. If we bring awareness to the regular themes that circle around our thoughts again and again we will soon begin to see our identifications. Identifications include, but are not limited to, possessions, knowledge, roles, likes, dislikes, creations, opinions, resentments, appearances, beliefs, positive or negative comparisons, addictions, attachments from the past or fantasies about the future. The related mind activities give us a sense of who we perceive ourself to be, which is the delusion. The truth is that who we really are is none of these things.

Let us work with an example of a man who identifies with being a husband. His wife divorces him, which means he is longer a husband. Does this mean he has disappeared or died? No, it does not. He is still there, which means he cannot be the role of husband that he identified with. Assume a person perceives himself or herself as having a weak body. Assume that they adjust their diet, exercise and train to strengthen the body making it stronger. The person is still there, but in a different physical form. Take somebody else who identifies with having a large house. They identify with being the person amongst their friendship group with the largest and most luxurious house. If their house gets burned down in an accident whilst they are away on holiday, does that person still exist? Of course they do, but they will be temporarily homeless. As you can see, all these things that people identify with are transient. These identifications cannot be who they really are. I once read that the cells within our own body get replaced every seven years, which implies that we are not even our own body. Therefore, our ego is deluded when it identifies with things and believes that it is who we are.

If we believe that we are who we think we are, that is not us. We cannot identify ourself with thought or speech. Who we are can only be known.

Paradoxically, who we are is not us personally, but shared with everybody and everything else, which means there is no real 'I'. There is only 'one'. The purpose of quality spiritual teachings is to connect us to that oneness.

To the ego, all identifications are viewed as beneficial. It believes that they are helping by adding something to our false sense of self. The truth is quite the contrary, because identifications reduce us rather than add to us. When we identify with something, we are constrained and vulnerable. Identifications take away our confidence, peace of mind, freedom, options and ability to respond creatively. The vision is to be capable of interacting and enjoying all form skilfully without getting identified with it. The capability to do this without identification is inherent within us, but the ego blocks it. Relating to form without identification is far more enjoyable because we are free from the background suffering of what we are identified with coming to an end, changing adversely or being taken away. When we reflect on our relationship to things, we find that we only usually identify with a few of them. The others we can enjoy with a sense of freedom. This shows that we are capable of relating to form in two modes; the first governed by the ego and the second governed by Presence. Over time, as we become more conscious, the identification with form reduces, leading to a lighter and happier relationship with life.

Delusion leads to suffering. The ego is always deluded, as it believes we are something that we are not. We have to be aware of the ego to be free from it. If our thoughts and actions are governed by the ego, we will be unskilful and suffer. If we allow Presence to govern our thoughts and actions, they will be skilful, which will lead to a peaceful existence. The ego tries to protect the things that we are identified with through control, as it is fearful of losing them and therefore losing itself. Through its delusion, it denies and fears the principle of impermanence that cannot be controlled. It reacts to this fear by worrying, controlling and being resistant to anybody or any situation that is a perceived threat to what it is identified with. The ego can also use human nature to strengthen itself. If you have children, you may be identified with your role as mother or father. Identification with this role motivates you to protect your children, which one could argue is a good thing, but without being governed through Presence even this can be unskilful in the form of the over-protective parent, controlling parent or boasting parent. The same is true of partners and anything else that we attach to and identify with. If we are ever aware of ourself trying to control things or people, this is a sign that the ego is active.

When we identify with opinions, the ego likes to create arguments and defend its position. Having opinions is fine and it can be interesting to debate them, but attachment to opinions leads to conflict. If the ego feels unsuccessful at controlling things to align with its identifications, it may resort to anger. Identification with possessions leads to obsessiveness and jealousy. Personally, I have experienced obsessiveness in relation to cars. When I was younger I was conditioned to believe that a car defined you and related to your sense of worth. I carried this into adulthood, which made me crave for new cars when the existing car I was driving was fine. Because I was so attached to my car, it resulted in me obsessing about whether I had closed the windows, locked the doors and so on. I was afraid of losing the car so much that my behaviours were irrational. You can purchase the most expensive, beautiful and luxurious car. If you identify with it, you will find that the suffering it causes will at best balance and usually outweigh the pleasure or benefit it provides. The same principle can be applied to any asset.

Sometimes we only know when we identify with something if it is removed, threatened or blocked in some way, which causes suffering. Where there is suffering, there is the ego and identification. I have experienced this myself when I have travelled to beautiful places with wonderful people around me. I became identified with what I had experienced without even knowing the identification had been created. This form of identification was multi-faceted and contained a number of components, including attachment to the pleasurable feelings of beautiful surroundings, the warm temperature and attachments to the companionship I shared with the people I had been staying with. The ego tricked me into believing that all these things are a part of who I am. The ego's operation and identification is often subtle. A little while before it was time to depart, usually a day or so before, I experienced suffering in the form of sadness as the ego tried to grasp onto something that had to be released.

I recall another time when I was identified with a pen! It was a good quality disposable pen and nothing too extravagant. The kind of pen you can buy in packs of three from a stationery store. I had always appreciated this particular pen, but never would have guessed that I was identified with it. One weekend, my son and I were watching videos and studying for a scuba diving trip we had planned. The pen was close by and whilst my son was watching the videos, he picked up the pen and started to bend back the clip that allowed me to secure it into my pocket. I became aware of my feelings of frustration and anger. After a minute or so I told him to leave the pen alone, took it from him and inspected the damage. I was disappointed and felt like a victim. A victim of pen abuse. I then confessed to my son that I was identified with the pen. He could sense my pain. He apologized and then offered me one of his pens from his bedroom. This is clearly a very subtle and insignificant example in the grand scheme of things, but it does illustrate how we unconsciously create identifications. The positive we can take with any example of identification is that every time we suffer, we have the opportunity to learn and progress. Suffering is a fine teacher and provides us with feedback. When we suffer, our job is to regain our connection with Presence and our true self. We do not become identified with or attach to anything when we are Present.

Once we are fully awakened, the ego is gone for good. All identifications are released, allowing us to respond creatively to every moment without any attachments or old patterns constraining us. Complete freedom is gained and our thinking is governed and initiated only when it is really needed. Even if we do not become fully awakened within this lifetime, we can still make significant progress. Some of the rewards from spiritual progress include higher levels of freedom, peace and happiness. Up until the point of full awakening, the ego will continue to take over from time to time and this reduces as we evolve. Getting to know the ego helps to reduce it. We must never resist or try to control the ego. This will only feed it and reinforce its existence. Instead, we develop a friendly curiosity towards its behaviour and impact. If we experience feelings that have a negative connotation, the ego is at work. These feelings may include, but are not limited to: anger, aversion, fear, annoyance, disquiet, vulnerability, embarrassment, sadness and yearning. All of these feelings are resisting the present moment. Wherever we find resistance to the present moment, we find the ego.

When the ego surfaces and causes problems, we can say to ourself, "that's the ego". It helps to label and gain some perspective on it. We can gain perspective because it is not who we are. For example, if we are feeling angry about a past situation when somebody did something that we believed was responsible for causing us pain, the ego may bring related thoughts to our attention in the form of images, movies and sounds associated with that person or situation. If this happens, we simply acknowledge them and mentally say, "the ego is creating those thoughts" or "the ego is creating those feelings". When we acknowledge the ego, we are instantly Present. This is analogous to acknowledging when we are lost in thought. We should give ourself a pat on the back when this happens as it shows that we have woken up.

Before we are fully awakened, we spend our days going to sleep and waking up. By 'going to sleep', I am referring to being lost in thought and by 'waking up' I am referring to awareness. We are lost in thought and then we regain awareness. Later, we may become lost in thought again and then we wake up and regain Presence. Our practice is to increase the amount of time when we are awake or Present. As we make progress, we literally see ourself coming in and out of awareness throughout the whole day. It is an empowering process and the more we are aware of being aware, the more skilful we become.

As we progress, we will begin to see the ego in others. Again, like our own ego, the egos in others do not need to be controlled or judged, just observed. If egos are judged, they are strengthened and grow, as the judgements reinforce the delusion that they actually exist. The ego is a concept we can use to help us understand the dysfunction of the mind. It is merely a process of dysfunctional thoughts and emotions taking place and there is nothing real or fixed about it. When we are aware of other people's egos, we protect ourself from getting wrapped up in their identifications, which means we remain Present. Only our ego can get wrapped up in the ego of another when we are lost in thought.

People can often spend much of the time talking about what they are identified with. It could be their children, pets, people they care about, jobs, acts of generosity, travel plans, where they live, difficulties from the past or any number of other things that occupy their lives. Talking about these subjects is a completely different experience when the communication flows out of Presence.

Instead of feeling depleting, the communication then feels nourishing and progressive. When it feels like we are listening to the same thing over and over again or if there is significant emotion behind it, this is the ego of the other person hijacking their thoughts and communication. In these situations, we must stay Present. We will protect ourself and may even wake the other person up in the process.

The ego likes to strengthen itself through thought, so solitude is not always an effective antidote. It is interesting to watch how the ego creates persistent identification-based thoughts about this or that relating to worries about the future or events from the past. Personally, I find it as challenging to transcend the ego whilst alone as I do when I am in the company of others. Here are some of the various guises in which the ego can manifest in our lives:

- Feeling superior or inferior to others.
- Feelings of fear, anxiety, expectation, regret, guilt or anger.
- Shyness and fear of attention from others.
- Craving.
- Unnecessary thoughts. Mental stories and fantasies.
- Suffering because something we identify with is lost or threatened.
- Absence of Presence and being lost in thought.
- Having perceived 'problems' with others.
- Unskilful thought, speech or action.

The ego operates within the realm of time and is always concerned with past and future. This is why Presence is the ultimate antidote. The ego will not activate and create suffering whenever we are grounded in the present moment. We should be curious about what, where, when, how and with whom our ego is manifesting. Understanding our own personal ego-based triggers and themes helps with this. We do not need to judge the ego, as this will strengthen it further. We simply observe what it is doing as a friendly and curious witness. This will create awareness, perspective and Presence.

We can find our own personal dramas or worries intensifying in situations that trigger fear or anxiety. The ego is afraid due to our past conditioning and its reaction may be to create thoughts that reinforce its identifications. The ego does this to strengthen itself given the perceived threat from the environment, regardless of whether the threat is real. It is afraid so it tries to make itself larger through thought with personal dramas and worries.

As our practice develops, we become aware of our two selves. The two selves are the ego and the Present-self. Our Present-self can be aware of the ego, but the ego is ignorant of the Present-self. In a similar way, our Present-self can influence the ego by reducing or suspending it, but the ego cannot influence the Present-self. Presence is ultimate and infinite and can only be influenced by itself. Over time, as we let go of our identification with roles, opinions, beliefs, memories, assets, addictions and other identifications, the ego reduces. We can still retain things, but we let go of identifying with them. The space that the ego once occupied with dysfunctional thoughts is replaced with a pure stillness. Ultimately, through full awakening, nothing remains of the ego and everything that remains is you.

This awareness of the two selves can be experienced within and outside of meditation. Meditation provides a good platform and the spaciousness for exploring the two selves as external distractions are kept to a minimum, allowing an inward focus. Every time we are lost in thought, we are experiencing a manifestation of the ego. Common examples include thoughts relating to the hindrances introduced earlier, including sensory desire, ill will, restlessness and worry. When we are aware of these thoughts, we are experiencing Presence being aware of the ego. This is liberating. It helps to gently remind ourself who we truly are, which is the awareness, not the ego. This de-personalises the ego and we connect with the Presence which is observing and holding it. This is analogous to holding an ice cube. The warmth of our hands, which represents Presence, melts the ice cube, which represents the ego. The ego should be held with a loving acceptance and understanding that it is based upon our past conditioning. Hating, resisting or discarding the ego reinforces and feeds it. We have to balance accepting the ego with taking responsibility for its reduction and ultimately its death.

To summarize, it is helpful to understand the ego if we want to reduce or release it. We must become the accepting, curious, silent witness for the ego. Understanding who we truly are helps us understand who we are not. Understanding who we are not helps us understand who we are. Who we are not is the ego. Who we are is Presence.

Responding to Difficult Feelings

We should bring awareness to the feelings associated with active hindrances. For example, if we are worrying, there may be a feeling of anxiety located somewhere in the body. It could be a sensation in the stomach, tension in the shoulders or somewhere else. If we are experiencing ill will towards ourself or somebody else, we might become aware of feelings of anger or frustration. The feelings we experience can be different from time to time and the way we experience them may also vary. The intention should be to bring acceptance to the feelings rather than resist them. Directly experiencing our difficult feelings in this way gives them attention, which is a more skilful route than escaping from them via our addictions. Attention and acceptance are what the feelings need to enable healing to take place.

Sometimes we are unaware of feelings, but aware of connected thoughts. For example, we might be aware of our thoughts being restless and jumping rapidly from here to there, but unaware of the feelings of restlessness within the body. If this happens, we can direct our awareness to the body and investigate. Once we have connected with the difficult feelings in the body and given them our attention for a while, it is then possible to respond and take the right action using our re-established connection with Presence.

Worldly Conditions

Another useful list from Buddhist teachings that covers hindrances are the worldly conditions. They consist of four opposites which are (i) gain and loss (ii) fame and infamy (iii) praise and blame and (iv) pleasure and pain. When the ego experiences these conditions, it reacts. It reacts by grasping onto what it believes are the positives (gain, fame, praise and pleasure) and resisting what it believes are the negatives (loss, infamy, blame and pain). The ego feeds off these conditions and uses them to create and reinforce identifications which are essential to its survival. The welcoming and resisting in this context are both forms of craving. Craving new positives or craving to retain the positives that we already have will lead to suffering because they are inherently subject to dissatisfaction and change. Resisting the negatives that arise also leads to suffering as the ego is wanting things to be different to how they are in that moment. When we are Present, we experience equanimity, which provides an inner state of peace and stability regardless of the worldly conditions that impact us. This allows us to enjoy worldly pleasures without craving them and to accept pain for what it really is, a natural and impermanent part of life. We may still have goals that we work towards with awareness and without getting lost in thought and creating identifications. We may also take responsibility and action to reduce our pain.

As part of our practice, it helps us to bring awareness to the ego when it reacts to the various conditions. For example, if a friend praises us for a good deed, we might be aware of thinking "I am amazing for doing that" or experience feelings of superiority. We might lose something that the ego identifies with such as a job or our favourite item of clothing and catch ourself blaming others or feeling angry about the situation. If the ego reacts, we must accept that it has reacted. We bring awareness to the ego, accept what it has done and then we take appropriate action to help the situation in that order. This is following the Four A's Cycle as described in Chapter Nine. By shining the light of awareness onto the ego in this way, accepting it and taking appropriate action, we reduce it and cultivate Presence.

We are at risk of getting blown around by these worldly conditions impacting others. When we are in the company of others and the worldly conditions trigger their egos, we must be Present in the same way that we would be Present for ourself. The Presence we connect with is the same as the Presence that others connect with because it is shared. So if you are Present when the egos of others are triggered through worldly conditions or other hindrances, you may help them to become Present. The intensity of your Presence needs to be adjusted to suit the situation and match the proportion of dysfunction of any egos that are active within that particular moment. This can be particularly challenging if you are amongst a dysfunctional group of people manifesting a collective ego.

The ego is incomplete and lacking by nature, which is the reason why it constantly craves for our experience to be different rather than accepting it in the present moment. Whenever the ego is operating, there will always be dissatisfaction of some description. There will be some gap that needs filling or aspect of our life that needs changing. We will never find peace and satisfaction when we are under the grip of the ego. On the contrary, when we are Present, we are complete. Every moment is complete and can be accepted exactly how it is whilst still having the option of taking action to change things in the future based on love for ourself or others.

The spiritual life is all about realizing the difference between the true essence of who we are and the ego. This creates a tension, which causes some necessary discomfort that is required for us to evolve in the same way that discomfort is required by our body to make it stronger. Through practice, we become skilled at residing in Presence and observing our ego. This realisation is purely conceptual. In absolute terms, there is no ego or true essence of *you*, but one vast and universal process of interrelated, changing conditions, that cover everything in existence, which is held by a formless intelligence, also known as Presence, consciousness, awareness or God. Whatever form the ego takes, all you need to do is to be the awareness in which it manifests and then anything else that is required for you to evolve from there will follow.

Triggering the Hindrances in Others

A wise friend of mine once told me that people are like smells. The more you are around them, the more of them rubs off onto you. Smells can be pleasant or unpleasant. If somebody who is manifesting a particular hindrance is in communication with somebody else that is lost in thought at the time, the hindrance may have a triggering effect. For example, if Person A is anxious whilst they are around Person B who is lost in thought, the ego of Person B may feed on some of that anxiety and manifest it. Have you ever been around somebody that is more anxious than you and found your anxiety level increasing as a result? If so, this is because you were lost in thought. This triggering effect happens frequently as we live in a society where many people are lost in thought most of the time. This also applies to collective hindrances that are impacting a group of any size, from a small gathering to a whole country. Presence protects us from our ego being activated and manifesting hindrances.

Hindrances during Sleep

Internal hindrances can be active when we are awake or asleep. This happens to an extent when we enter dream-like states during the day if we are lost in thought as well as when we are asleep at night. Even during our physical sleep, the ego is busy fuelling dreams that reinforce our identifications by creating a different version of the self-referential reality that we experience during the day. It is impossible to prove whether anything we experience during the day or in our dreams is absolutely real. All we know for sure is that it appears to be real to us at the time we experience it. If you dream you are flying through the sky like Superman, then the related thoughts and feelings are real thoughts and feelings. Your *experience* of the dream is real. You may also experience feelings of excitement. Those feelings are real too. When our minds are completely still in deep sleep during certain periods of the night, the ego subsides, which makes deep sleep helpful for spiritual progress. Our sleep quality and dream content tell us a lot about the state of our ego.

Nightmares are a form of suffering. If we are dreaming about something that is creating unpleasant feelings such as frustration, anger, vulnerability or grief, we will be suffering during that dream. These feelings may then unfold into the day. We may wake up on a morning and feel anxious, but not know why. Or we wake up feeling anxious and can recall an unpleasant dream that the feeling may have been linked with. This is why people may say, "I've woken up on the wrong side of the bed." Sometimes, it can then take a few hours for those feelings to subside as we wake up and the mind let's go of the unconscious thought process. The suffering we experience through our dreams has many things in common with the suffering we experience through events during the day. One of the things that both forms of suffering have in common is that they teach us. When we suffer, we are reminded about our identifications and the impact of them through the ego. Whether the reminder is known consciously or unconsciously is irrelevant for progress to take place. The mind reminds itself of the impact of creating and reinforcing identifications and learns from that. Nightmares must not be induced like any form of suffering, but if we experience them naturally, we can be grateful for them, as they will teach us.

POINTS FOR REFLECTION

- The challenges we face during meditation or any other activity resulting in a lack of concentration and being lost in thought will be due to one or more hindrances, which are (i) sensory desire (ii) ill will (iii) sloth and torpor (iv) restlessness-worry and (v) doubt.

- One result of becoming more Present is that we naturally make a transition from seeking sensory pleasure towards seeking contentment.

- Sensory pleasures consumed without awareness lead to intoxication, which generates excessive thinking and a high, which is outside of our accessible field of awareness.

- We can delight in pleasure or allow it to intoxicate us. When we are Present, we delight in pleasure. When we are lost in thought, the pleasure will intoxicate us. True pleasure can only be experienced when we are Present.

- The ego is the ultimate hindrance to Presence.

- Identifications that constitute the ego can be positive or negative.

- Identifications include possessions, knowledge, roles, likes, dislikes, personal creations, opinions, appearance, beliefs, long-standing resentments, positive or negative comparisons, addictions, attachments from the past or fantasies about the future.

- The ego wants to protect the things that we are identified with, as it is fearful of losing them and therefore losing itself.

- We must always take responsibility for the ego causing problems and learn from our mistakes.

- We should never resist or try to control the ego. This will only feed it and reinforce its existence. Instead, we develop a friendly curiosity towards its behaviour and impact on our thoughts.

- Wherever we find resistance of the present moment, we find the ego.

- Ultimately, through awakening, nothing remains of the ego and everything that remains is you.

- We have to balance accepting the ego with taking responsibility for its reduction and ultimately its death.

- When we acknowledge the ego, we are Present.

- As we progress, we begin to see the ego in others. The ego in others does not need to be controlled or judged, just observed and accepted.

- Only our ego can get wrapped up in the ego of another when we are lost in thought.

- The vision is to be capable of interacting and enjoying all form skilfully without becoming identified with it.

- Understanding who we truly are helps us understand who we are not. Understanding who we are not helps us understand who we truly are.

- Identifications take away our confidence, peace of mind, freedom, options and ability to respond creatively.

- When we suffer, the next step is to regain our connection with Presence and our true self.

OPTIONAL LEARNING ACTIVITIES

- Bring awareness to the repetitive themes that circle around in your thoughts again and again. Through doing this, you will begin to understand what you are identified with.

- When the ego surfaces and causes you problems, you can say to yourself "that's the ego". It helps to label the ego to gain perspective from it.

- Use meditation to bring awareness to the two selves through the awareness of thoughts. The two selves are the Present-self and the ego. The Present-self creates skilful thoughts and the ego creates unskilful thoughts.

- Be curious about what, where, when, how and with whom your ego is manifesting. Understand your own personal ego-based triggers and themes.

- Regularly remind yourself who you truly are, which is your awareness, not the ego.

Chapter Six

Simplicity

A relationship exists between simplicity and Presence. Simplifying our life helps us to cultivate Presence and Presence equips us to manage complexity. If we believe things are too complex, we must work to simplify them. If we use an iceberg as a symbol for simplicity, the tip of the iceberg above the sea level represents our external simplicity, which covers our visible life, including all our different roles, relationships, possessions and so on. The much larger part of the iceberg, below the sea level, is our internal simplicity, which is measured positively by how peaceful our minds are and measured negatively by how much we are lost in thought. These thoughts are closely linked with our emotions, which are also underneath the iceberg. The two parts of the iceberg are different, which explains why one part of the iceberg can appear simple whilst the other part appears complex.

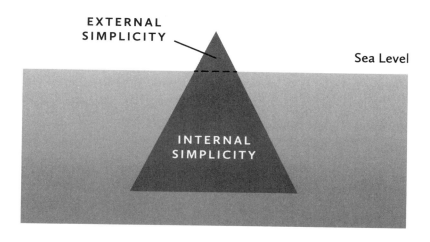

The Simplicity Iceberg

Balancing Simplicity with Wisdom & Compassion

Our lives consist of a number of roles and these roles influence the overall complexity of our experience. Examples of common roles are partner, son, mother, homeowner, employee and friend. The roles relate to themes of activities. For example, the role of homeowner may include activities such as cleaning, maintenance, paying bills and so on. If we are looking at removing complexity from our life, it can help to create a list of our various roles and activities. From there, we can decide what roles or activities can be simplified or removed. We should always remove or add complexity to our life consciously. This means carefully considering the consequences before we embrace or release various responsibilities and activities.

If we own more than we need, whether that be homes, cars, clothes, gadgets or anything else, our life will be more complex than it needs to be. Sometimes it is necessary to let go of activities rather than assets, such as seeing certain people or visiting places that lead to us becoming lost in thought. Letting go can be an emotional journey and we may consider reducing our life complexity gradually to give us time to integrate the changes. The ideal method of simplification is to start with removing the activities or assets that are causing harm. This requires courage and skill as it often means releasing our addictions, which is covered in the next chapter.

We can experiment by reducing complexity and then observing changes in our levels of Presence. For example, we can simplify our work, let go of some assets or create some space in our schedule so that we can take more time over things and complete our activities mindfully. When we purchase products, we can consider their level of simplicity as well as their other attributes such as price and functionality. Ironically, we may find that to simplify our life, it is necessary to carry additional complexity during the transition. For example, simplifying our work may introduce additional activities for a period of time as we find a new job or change how we approach our existing job.

Planning helps to simplify our life. We can take time out on a regular basis to stop and create a list of prioritized activities. The human mind can only spin so many plates concurrently without support from a tool such as a to-do list. Simplifying our lives is an ongoing challenge. Things change and before we know it the simplicity that we cultivated is taken away and we have to replan and reconfigure.

The drive for simplicity must be balanced with wisdom. Before making a decision to simplify part of our life, we should forecast what the impact might be on ourself and others. We may need to be creative and work towards simplicity in a different way or at a different time. Sometimes it is right to consciously accept complexity for a period of time and make changes later. If we try and simplify an area of our life too early, it will end up achieving the opposite and adding complexity rather than removing it. I have been keen to let go of owning a car for a number of years, but my work situation and parental responsibilities mean that my life would be more complex logistically without one. If the conditions are right to let go of the car in the future, then I will do so. It is a matter of staying receptive and taking the right opportunities to simplify our life at the appropriate times.

If we have a complex situation that needs to remain for a while, we can look to create simplicity within it. For example, if we have complex travel arrangements, we can simplify them by having periods of time in Presence and letting go of multi-tasking. If we are driving, we may just focus on the driving and nothing else. If we are sitting in an airport waiting for a flight, then we may simply wait and let go of doing anything else. If we are walking from here to there, we may give the walking and the surroundings our full attention. This adds pockets of simplicity and meditation, which results in an overall reduction in complexity. Sometimes, we need to add complexity to our life for good reason and this should always be introduced consciously.

It is a common phenomenon that when we become more Present, we may end up doing less. We move from a stressed state of rushing around and filling our time to inserting more space in-between our activities and tackling them at a pace that lends itself more to being Present. As a consequence, the things that we do will be of higher quality, more creative, powerful, skilful and aligned with what is needed. Life becomes lighter, smoother and more enjoyable. Less is often more. Finally, having more space in our life means that we are much better placed to be receptive and respond to the needs of others allowing ourself to be more generous with our time and energy.

Simple & Repetitive Activities

The vast majority of life is filled with simple and repetitive activities. Examples include brushing our teeth, waiting in a queue, visiting the toilet, falling to sleep or washing the dishes. Those who are working on being Present have a very different relationship with simple activities because they view them as opportunities to practise. Every simple activity can be used to become mindful of our inner experience and what is entering through the senses. It is an opportunity to gain freedom from thought for a while and become peaceful. Sometimes, that peacefulness creates enjoyment and enthusiasm. The simpler our life, the less external input there will be to stimulate thought, which provides greater opportunity for our minds to become still.

The other option and default for many, which I do not recommend, is to allow ourself to be lost in thought during simple activities. It is easy to get lost in thought during these times because there is nothing much to think about that relates to what we are doing. Brushing our teeth does not require a great deal of thought. Once we have selected our clothes for the day, getting dressed does not require a great deal of thought. These activities have become habitual and can be undertaken with little or no conscious thought. If thought is not governed during these activities, it jumps straight into the past or future and the ego forces it to become self-referential, which is a one-way ticket to suffering. The quality of the output from the simple activity will be reduced and any opportunity to be at peace and enjoy what we are doing is removed. So our goal should be to stay Present during simple activities.

Repetitive activities are only repetitive when we are lost in thought. When we are Present, they are naturally fresh. Things only feel repetitive when we are thinking about times when we have done something similar before. Although we may be doing the same thing conceptually, the detail within the experience will always be unique. We never have exactly the same experience brushing our teeth on one day to the next. The differences include the physical movement of the hands, the taste of the toothpaste, the water flowing into the sink, thoughts that enter our mind and changes to our posture. These things may appear identical on the surface, but when we examine the detail, there are differences. We can remove the repetition in repetitiveness through awareness.

Many religions recommend a simple life to enable spiritual progress and simplicity is often factored into religious environments including ashrams and monasteries. The intention is to provide simplicity in the surroundings and daily schedule practised by the residents. I have visited and stayed in numerous ashrams and monasteries. Each visit reminded me to keep life simple and that life does not need to be lived in a way that Western culture encourages us, which is towards more and more complexity. It is not essential to live in an ashram or monastery to make progress and lead a simple life, but visiting for a few days or weeks is an inspiring way of learning how things can be arranged differently. Many practices from an ashram or monastery can be adjusted and integrated into a Western lifestyle. Examples include meditation, chanting, silence, mindfulness during simple work activities, yoga and limiting the use of technology. It is possible for us all to make our life simpler through creativity and discipline.

To create a simpler life, we can replace a few activities that require thought with activities that require little or no thought. We are not aiming to completely remove thought from our lives, as thought is required for us to function in the world. Thought is fine as long as it is manifested from a state of Presence where it will be imbued with quality, wisdom and love.

Simplicity & Assets

Reducing the amount of assets that we own reduces complexity and the need to think. If we own something, the mind can raise various questions, including, "Where is it located?", "Do I want to use it today?", "Shall I take it with me?", "Does it need maintaining?", "Do I need a new one?", "What will happen if it gets damaged?", "Is it safe?", "Have I paid too much for it?", "How can I sell it?", "How much will it cost to run?", "Who have I lent it to?", "Does it need charging?", "How did that dent or scratch get there?" All of these questions require thought and may stimulate emotion. The more we own, the more thinking is required. Reducing the amount we own does need balancing with our needs and the needs of those that are dependent upon us. In a family situation where children are involved, this requires careful consideration. I recall removing the TV from my home whilst I had responsibility for my son for part of the week. I needed to manage the situation delicately, checking to see how he felt about it and ensuring that he could be entertained via alternative means. I would have kept the TV for longer if I predicted that its removal had been harmful in some way. As it turned out, letting go of it was beneficial to both of us.

The Simplicity Paradox

There is an interesting paradox linking complexity, simplicity and Presence. We can create a simpler life to make it easier for us to become more Present. The more Present we become, the more skilled we will be at managing complexity. It is fine for life to contain conscious complexity and problematic for it to contain unconscious complexity. Conscious complexity is complexity that is added to our life wisely. Unconscious complexity is added unintentionally or ignorantly by the ego when we are lost in thought.

Successful Presence practitioners balance simplicity and complexity. For example, they may outwardly face the world and perform a complex task in a complex environment and then return to simple tasks or stillness within a simple environment before reappearing again. The Buddha was famous for this. Whilst he entered challenging environments and helped people with complex situations, his life also contained simplicity, providing balance. He was known to take refuge in nature from time to time.

Planned meditation provides a gateway into simplicity. We sit down in a quiet environment and close our eyes. We then focus on our breath and allow ourself to become Present. There is a real simplicity in that. The ego tries to make meditation complex by triggering emotions, getting lost in self-referential thought, craving and creating dramas, but once we let go of all this unnecessary action, we are left with a very simple experience. Creating time for meditation is creating time for simplicity.

Let us return to the paradox. Creating a simpler life will make it easier for us to become more Present and the more Present we are, the more skilled we will become at managing complexity. This is because when we are Present, we find simplicity in complexity. Any complex activity or situation becomes extremely simple when it is experienced within the present moment. In the present moment, there is no past or future to be concerned with and all that is required is concentration on the action you are taking at the time, which may be no action. There is nothing complex about the present moment. Complexity is created through thought and the overlay of self and time introducing past and future. When we are lost in thought, we create complexity out of simplicity. When we are Present, we bring simplicity to complexity.

As well as experiencing simplicity within complexity, it is also possible to experience complexity within simplicity. Creating simplicity within complexity through Presence is helpful. Bringing complexity into simplicity by getting lost in thought is unhelpful. We may be presented with a simple situation and our egos will make that situation complex through thinking. This can happen with human interactions. When we are Present in the company of others, communication is simple and straightforward. We make it complicated when we become lost in thought and add comparisons, judgements, create stories and then try to fit people into our internal perception of our world. Our internal perception may feel real to us, but it is not real in reality. Everybody else's perception is different and nobody has a complete view of the true reality of any situation. We experience different worlds within the same world. We experience a very limited, personalized view of a tiny subset of what is possibly out there and the rest of our experience is mind generated.

Another example of creating complexity out of simplicity is when an unconscious person gets caught out in the rain without an umbrella or raincoat. It is actually quite a simple situation. They are wet, cold and need to take action to find shelter or carry on moving towards their destination. Instead of accepting the simplicity of the situation, they may make it complex with complaints about the weather, blaming others, blaming God, judging themselves for not having an umbrella, worrying about how they might look when they arrive at their destination or worrying about catching a cold. All of this thought is completely unnecessary at that moment in time and prevents them from accepting the situation peacefully. Acceptance of any situation introduces simplicity and drives appropriate action if it is needed.

If we have the skills to write, we may consider writing a book. We may believe this is a complex task, but it is actually quite simple when we are Present. The content of the book flows from inside of us out onto the page or computer screen with little or no thought. The same goes for other things that are produced when we are truly creative. Things do not need to be complex. We choose to add complexity through thought, which is generated by our egos and based in the realm of time. With the book example, if we let go of time whilst we are writing, any concerns about how long it might take, whether it will be published or whether it will be complete by a certain date are relinquished. Timelessness helps to ease any creative processes, as we are focused and not constrained through emotions created from worries about the past or future. We may want to allocate a certain amount of time to creating things, planning and reflecting. During these activities we may check in on the time periodically for practical purposes. Our relationship with time as we create can end there.

There are certain activities where we are naturally aware of our experience with little conscious effort and other activities that lead to us becoming lost in thought. For example, we may always be aware of feeling water against our skin and the sound of the water whilst washing our hands, but get lost in thought whilst brushing our teeth.

Through analysing our simple activities, we soon learn which activities are the ones that require a conscious effort to remain Present. We may also recognize common thought patterns and themes that occur when we are lost in thought, which can be used as prompts to regain Presence if we notice them. It can be easier to select one or two activities to work on at any given time rather than trying to transform them all at once. Ideally, before we start the activity, we remember to become Present, which may mean anchoring to the breath or other bodily sensations. Then, once we are undertaking the activity, we remain Present by keeping a small amount of attention on the breath or another anchor. This keeps us alert and aware of our direct experience. If thoughts or feelings occasionally pop into our awareness, we simply let them pass and re-anchor to the breath or another source. We can also use props to remind ourself to become Present prior to our activities. In the teeth brushing example, placing a small object beside our toothbrush can remind us to become Present before we pick it up.

Eckhart Tolle's Modalities of Awakened Doing[4] referenced in Chapter Ten can be applied to simple and repetitive activities. If it is not possible to bring acceptance to a simple activity, then we may need to stop doing it. Most of the time it is possible to accept and surrender to activities, which allows us to complete them peacefully. We may even go on to enjoy some of the activities that we brought acceptance to. What starts out as a simple, repetitive, unpleasant activity is transformed into something meditative, peaceful and enjoyable. Part of our practice should be to accept some of the simple and repetitive activities that we currently resist. We can make a start by working on one or two. This raises our confidence and motivation to go on and do the same with others. A side advantage of this approach is that we will be less likely to multi-task, thus increasing the quality of the activity and any output or results that we create. For example, a meal that is prepared mindfully by somebody who is Present at the time will be far more enjoyable to consume than a meal thrown together in haste and with disregard by somebody who is lost in thought. When you are receptive, you can feel the Presence or love within the creations and behaviours of others.

Technology & Messaging

The amount of time people are spending using digital devices, including communication via electronic messages such as emails, texts, and social media, continues to increase, so it is relevant to consider this within our practice. Some make bland statements, advising people to use their devices less and have periods of time when they should be switched off altogether. This can be helpful to align with a personal requirement such as needing the freedom to concentrate on a specific task, having some space or aligning with social etiquette. Turning our devices off is not a hard and fast prerequisite for being Present. The influencing factor for being Present is not about how much we use our devices, but the consciousness we bring to their usage. We can bring Presence into everything, including technology and messaging. Presence may lead us to continue to use a device, switch it off for a while, replace it, use it more or get rid of it altogether based on whatever is skilful at the time.

If we respond to messages in a reactive way, this can cause problems. This happens when we are lost in thought about the past or future whilst we are typing. If we reflect on our level of Presence immediately after sending a message, we can bring awareness to how conscious our usage of the device was at that point in time. If we go back and read the message we sent, its quality will also signify how Present we were when we typed it. A typical reactive response may be to reply to a message quickly and habitually to tick the, 'I've replied' box, and move on to something else that our ego believes to be more important, based on its deluded agenda. When we are lost in thought, patterns are used to create the content for the message based on old habits and circumstances that may be irrelevant in the current context. Responding with Presence means that the response is creative and relevant for the moment in which we operate.

I explain many times how anchoring to the breath is a great way to stay Present. This technique can be applied to anything, including the use of technology. As I am writing this chapter, I am anchored to my breath, which keeps me Present and I make an effort to do the same when I am using my phone and other technology. I facilitated an exercise on a mindfulness course, asking attendees to use their phones whilst keeping a small amount of awareness anchored to the breath. Positive results were reported, including freedom from judging the person they were in communication with, higher levels of concentration and a deeper interpretation and feeling of empathy whilst reading messages. I invite you to embrace your device usage as an opportunity to practise Presence and experience the benefits for yourself.

A decision to use any kind of technology needs to be made consciously. Many people will switch on the TV or use their devices without consciously deciding to do so. They are operating on autopilot. When technology is used in this way, the user is simply following a habitual pattern or reacting to an addictive cycle. Right action can only be taken when we are Present. The only time a mobile phone or any other device should be used is if the user consciously decides it is appropriate at the time. This is using technology consciously.

If we do not use technology consciously, it will feel as though it is using us. It is not using us at all, but what is happening is that we are allowing ourself to be governed by the information flowing into our device and ultimately our mind. We may not be able to control all the information that is presented to us, but we can influence it greatly by configuring our technology to deliver content that helps us to stay Present and to let go of content that hinders us. If the content is regularly activating our ego and we do not have the capacity to stay Present whilst viewing it, then we should consider reconfiguring our device to let go of the content. This is common on social media sites where content uploaded encourages us to make positive or negative comparisons and strengthens the ego. The ego loves social media. It is one of its favourite junk foods. Social media, is fine and can be beneficial as long as our interactions with it are imbued with Presence.

Content delivered through our devices that we use for the purpose of intoxication should be avoided. There are many examples of this type of content with two of the common genres being pornography and violence. The creation of this type of content is often rooted in craving. Many people create, produce and feature in these films, videos and audio streams because they are escaping from their own pain. This content is created to escape from pain and used to escape from pain. It is acting as a link in an interconnected mesh that connects and feeds people's addictions.

Through our spiritual practice, we have the option to break that link, release our addictions and remove ourself from reinforcing the addictions of others. Experiencing pleasure is an enjoyable part of life as long as it is free from craving and intoxication. Intoxication occurs when we lose ourself in the pleasurable experiences. The moment this happens, we are causing ourself or others harm and creating or reinforcing an addiction. Enjoying pleasure whilst we are Present, however, is harmless and delightful, and can nurture us.

If we enjoy using technology, this can be integrated into our spiritual development with ease by accessing content through quality websites or mobile apps. I often use time on public transport and in hotels to learn from some great teachers who use online channels to reach those with an appetite to learn. Mobile devices can also be used for journalling and reflection which enable us to integrate what we have learned from teachings into our own personal experience. We may enjoy all the benefits that technology brings and remain Present by ensuring that we take responsibility for configuring it skilfully, using it consciously and safely.

Waiting

We have many opportunities to wait for things. We wait in queues at the supermarket or for public transport. We wait at traffic lights. We wait for the kettle to boil. When most people need to wait for a short period of time, they will drop into a habitual cycle and react by doing something. For some, a little voice inside their head will say "Don't waste time, do something!" Many people go straight for their phone. There will be no conscious choice involved and their minds and bodies will react with a pre-programmed habit of taking the phone out of their pocket or bag, checking for new content, making calls, posting to social media sites or sending messages.

Waiting is a golden opportunity to regain or sustain Presence. Unless there is some urgent need to do something, we can use waiting to become aware of our senses, acknowledging what is around us, connecting with our breath and body, observing our thoughts or checking in with how we are feeling. We do not always have to be doing something. If we wait without doing, we can enable being. Then once we have finished waiting, we can continue doing and carry the being into the doing. This means we are doing with Presence. If we take the opportunity to become Present whilst waiting for a meal to arrive in a restaurant, we will enhance our interaction with the waiter or waitress when they visit the table, increase our awareness of the meal and be better placed to enjoy it. A meal or anything else for that matter cannot be truly enjoyed when we are lost in thought. If we use an opportunity to become Present whilst waiting in traffic, we will be safer and more likely to enjoy our driving experience once the traffic is moving again. So we cultivate being whilst we wait and then integrate the being into the doing when we resume our activities.

We can engineer opportunities to wait by taking brief pauses between activities. For example, if we have sent an email, we can wait a few seconds before moving on to the next task. If we have finished driving, we can wait for a minute before getting out of the car. During a frantic day, we might believe that the best thing is to do as much as possible without pausing. In my experience, it is often the case that the slower we go, the faster we go. We may temporarily slow down by interspersing our activities with pauses. Then by doing this and integrating more Presence into the doing, we become more effective and achieve more in less time. What we do is of higher quality and has fewer issues. This is the paradox of being able to speed up by slowing down.

We can establish a practice where we can use waiting as an opportunity to become Present and turn waiting into a meditation. To begin with, we can practise this in specific situations such as the supermarket queue or waiting in a line of traffic. We can place our attention outwards towards our surroundings or inwards towards our personal experience. A good start is to use one instance of waiting each day to practise being Present. This may feel difficult to start with if we are the type of person who fills most of their time with activity. We may even experience some irrational guilt if we just wait and hear a voice inside our head telling us that we should be doing something. If this process feels uncomfortable, then we can tell ourself the truth, that is, when we resume our activities, we will be far more effective and likely to get more of the right things done well. A side benefit of this practice is that we never need to complain about waiting again as it allows us to view waiting as a gift. We can be grateful if somebody or something causes us to wait. The person or situation has provided us with an opportunity to meditate.

Assets, De-cluttering & Physical Spaciousness

A simpler life makes it easier to stay Present and one of the things that influences simplicity is the amount of assets you own. This ranges from large physical items, such as property or cars, to smaller items such as books and crockery. Assets may also be non-physical, including investments or downloaded files on our computers. The assets we own take space and often require thought, which means they carry an overhead. Clearly, we need a certain amount of things to operate in the world and meet our needs. Over time, as we become more Present and content, we find that we need less to live happily. Then, if more is presented to us, in whatever form, we are free to enjoy it without becoming attached. It is then fine to let it go and be content without it once again, if that is what is required of us.

The challenge we face is to balance our needs with simplicity. Should we reduce what we own through force? No, simplicity should never be forced. Instead, we allow simplicity to evolve naturally through understanding how our assets help or hinder us. Sometimes having the assets is fine, but our relationship with them is dysfunctional. This is particularly the case if we identify with assets, believing that they make us who we are, which is the ego at work. People do this with all sorts of things, including significant items such as houses and cars to smaller items such as mobile phones or items of clothing. When we identify with an asset, it will cause us suffering in various ways through loss, fear of loss, obsession, possessiveness, envy, comparisons or disappointment.

Assets can serve us for a time, but they will never ultimately satisfy us. Even if we have something that we think is perfect for a while, it will ultimately cause us suffering if we identify with it. Either the asset will change or our relationship with it will change. Either way, every asset provides temporary satisfaction at best. It is identification with the asset that causes the problem rather than the asset itself. As I mentioned, increasing our connection with the formless provides perspective on form, including assets and allows us to have a lighter relationship with them. They may still be important to us within their context, but relatively important compared to the absoluteness of Presence, which is the only thing that is ultimately satisfying and reliable. Our phone may be very important in the context of making an important call or sending a message, but in the grand scheme of things and from the perspective of Presence, it is only relatively important. To be ultimately satisfied, we need to be looking in the right realm, which means being connected with nothing rather than craving for something.

There is another paradox here. We need to take responsibility for our assets and respect their importance whilst at the same time realizing their insignificance. We should maintain and look after the things that are dear to us and serve us well, but not identify with them. Relationships are also assets which can be viewed in the same light. This balances responsibility with lightness. It is possible and wise to hold both views. You can successfully hold the relative view in one hand and the absolute view in the other. Something is relatively important whilst being absolutely insignificant. As a general rule, when we learn to hold both of these views simultaneously, our lives become smoother and happier. Lightness is evident within our interactions in the world and through this we become more positively effective.

Creating space within our environments can help reduce thinking and also enable mental spaciousness. Examples of environments include our home or place of work. This link between physical space and mental space also applies to temporary environments, which we occupy, such as a hotel room. If the environment contains more assets than we actually need or is arranged chaotically, then we will need to think more in order to operate within it. If we are trying to locate something in a cupboard that is overflowing with items that have been inserted without care and attention, there is a fair chance that we are going to become stressed looking for it. If the cupboard contains fewer items and is arranged mindfully, then there will be little thought and no stress involved in locating the item. This all sounds very simple and it is. If we create an environment whilst being lost in thought, being in that environment will lend itself to being lost in thought. If we create an environment whilst we are Present, then being in that environment will lend itself to being Present. You may resonate with this if you reflect on environments you have created or entered in the past and the impact they had on your peace of mind and general functioning. This applies equally to digital environments, including how we arrange virtual items on our phone or laptop.

Creating physical space within our environments rather than having them cluttered is helpful for our practice. Physical space is a gateway into Presence because there is nothing there within that space. We cannot see anything within physical space. There is nothing to label. There is just space or emptiness. When we give that space our attention, it leads us into Presence. The same goes for silence. It can often be easier to become Present when there is less to experience. This is why people have been meditating for years with their eyes closed and in silence. This is also why the vastness and space provided by nature leaves us feeling so good. It removes distraction and reduces the amount of thinking required. Then, through that stillness of the mind, we can enter a state of Presence. The ultimate intention is to become Present with the option to let go of thought at any time regardless of what is going on around us. In the meantime, whilst we are progressing, the use of meditation, physical space, silence, nature or other gateways as specified in this book and elsewhere are training aids that we can use to help us along the way.

Streamlining

It is easy to become lost in thought when we are doing too much. We end up squeezing so many activities into the day that we force ourself into auto-pilot mode. The more things we do, the faster we need to go to complete them. When we speed up, it is more challenging to stay aware, and we need awareness to respond skilfully to our experience. Once we go over our personal speed limits, we are no longer Present and our minds fall back into old patterns. Sometimes these patterns serve us, but when they are irrelevant to the new context, they cause problems. For example, if we are not taking quality time to listen to somebody and rushing them along, we may end up concluding that they are telling us something that we have guessed at rather than understanding what they intended to communicate. If we are rushing to drive somewhere, we may go too quickly and be less likely to respond effectively to the demands of the road conditions.

It is possible to do things quickly with Presence if we are aware and honest with ourself about our own personal speed limit. We can streamline our life so that we do less and this will help us to bring more Presence and quality into the activities that remain. The first method for streamlining is to stop doing the things that we should not be doing. By this, I mean we stop doing the things that are hindering us or causing harm. The second method, which is actually a variant of the first, is to ask the question: "Does this really need doing?" If we are doing something that we do not need to do, then the ego will always be governing the action. Activities that are governed by the ego can be identified, as they involve craving. It is surprising how many unnecessary things we do in our life to satisfy our ego. For example, we may have enough clothes, but we go shopping for more. Our home is tidy enough to live in and we clean it unnecessarily. We are tired and our body needs to rest, but we choose to exert ourselves. We have enjoyed watching a nourishing programme on TV but then spend time watching something else that depletes us. Streamlining means facing into our addictions, the ego, feeling and releasing the underlying emotional pain that is driving our unnecessary activities. If we are doing or planning to do something, but not quite sure why, there is often an addiction influencing the activity. For most, streamlining should be a gradual practice. If we are creating suffering with this practice or any of the other practices introduced in this book, then we are doing too much and should do less.

Simplicity of the Present Moment

In absolute terms, the complexity we feel is not a result of the things we do, but a result of our reactive thoughts about those things. When we are Present and undertaking any activity, our minds are clear and concentrated. Everything we need in terms of right action is presented to us and life is remarkably simple.

A complex task always breaks down into a number of simple tasks, which can be approached with Presence. An essential part of our practice is to enable Presence through these simple tasks. They can be anything from brushing our teeth to writing an email. Even a complex email can be broken down into a number of taps on the keyboard or discrete sections of thought, which can manifest simply through Presence. Simplifying our life may help, but the ultimate opportunity for simplification is through residing in the present moment. The mini breathing meditation introduced in chapter two is a great way of initiating this.

POINTS FOR REFLECTION

- Simplifying our life supports the cultivation of Presence and Presence equips us to manage complexity.

- We must always consider the consequences before removing or adding complexity to our life.

- We can remove the repetition in repetitiveness through awareness.

- When simplifying our life, we start by removing the activities or assets that are causing ourself or others harm.

- Reducing the amount of items that we own can reduce complexity and the need to think.

- We can simplify our lives by changing or letting go of unnecessary or unhelpful assets, relationships or activities.

- We should consider reducing our life complexity gradually to give us time to integrate the changes.

- Having more space in our life means that we are far better placed to respond to the needs of others.

- Every simple activity can be used for us to become mindful of our inner experience and what is entering through the senses.

- Any complex activity or situation becomes extremely simple when it is executed within the present moment.

- Complexity is created through thought and the overlay of self and time bringing in the past and future.

- In the present moment, there is no past or future to be concerned with and all that is required is concentration on the action you are taking at the time, which may be no action.

- Timelessness helps make our creations effortless, as we are not constrained through emotions created from thoughts about the past or future.

- As well as creating simplicity within complexity (helpful), it is also possible to create complexity within simplicity (unhelpful).

- When we are lost in thought, we create complexity out of simplicity. When we are Present, we may find simplicity within complexity.

- The only time a phone or any other device should be used is if the user consciously decides it is appropriate at the time.

- If we do not use technology consciously, then it will feel as though it is using us.

- The influencing factor for being Present is not about how much we are using devices, but the consciousness we bring to their usage.

- Our internal perception of the world may feel real to us, but it is not real in reality. We all experience different worlds within the same world.

- Waiting is a golden opportunity to regain or sustain Presence.

- An essential part of our practice is to enable Presence through simple activities.

- Streamlining means facing into our addictions, the ego, and experiencing the underlying emotional pain that is driving our unnecessary activities.

- If we are doing or planning to do something, but not quite sure why, there is often an addiction influencing the activity.

- Our internal perception may feel real to us, but it is not real in reality. We experience a very limited, personalized view of a tiny subset of what is actually out there and the rest of our experience is mind generated.

- To be ultimately satisfied, we need to be looking in the right realm, which means being connected with nothing rather than craving for something.

- The ultimate opportunity for simplification is through Presence.

OPTIONAL LEARNING ACTIVITIES

- Ask yourself if your life is too complex for you to experience in a way that allows you to stay Present for a reasonable amount of time. If it is, then consider external simplification.

- List all your various roles and activities. From there, you can decide what roles or activities can be simplified or removed.

- Take time out on a regular basis to stop and create a list of prioritized activities.

- Add simplicity to situations by doing one thing at a time.

- Select one or two simple activities and the next time you complete them, anchor to the breath or a bodily sensation throughout. Notice how the experience changes for you.

- Consider donating, selling or recycling your personal assets, which you do not need.

- Create physical space in your home by de-cluttering.

- Bring awareness to when you are adding unnecessary complexity to situations. For example, unnecessary thinking when interacting with others.

- Next time you are using a mobile device such as a phone or tablet, bring full consciousness to its use by staying anchored to the breath or bodily sensations.

- Engineer opportunities to wait and become Present by taking brief pauses between activities.

- Establish a practice where you can use waiting as an opportunity to become Present and turn waiting into a meditation.

Chapter Seven

Addictions

If we gain freedom from our addictions, we will become Present. This makes understanding addictions and taking responsibility to release them an essential part of our practice. There are many definitions that attempt to explain what an addiction is. Here is my personal definition:

Addictions are unskilful, compulsive thought
patterns that can only be released through Presence.

We can feel as though addictions are controlling us, with the 'us' referring to our deluded sense of self or ego. When we bring awareness to our addictions, we transcend them. For example, a smoker can be viewed in two ways. The first view is that they are a smoker, which is a role they have taken on, one which is causing them harm. The second view relates to the true essence of them, which knows that smoking is harmful and wishes for them to stop. When a person connects to their true essence, they gain a wise perspective on the addiction, allowing them to make it manageable through compartmentalization, and seeing that it is an addiction and not who they truly are. Any fixed view or judgement of self is illusory, as our minds and bodies are constantly changing. We are not the same person from one moment to the next and we have the power to be creative in every moment. With this knowledge, we can be empowered to make positive changes and release our addictions.

If we were to talk about addictions to the average man or woman on the street, some of the common things that come to mind are cigarettes, drugs, alcohol, sex, chocolate and shopping. The truth is that addictions are much wider than this, which is why my definition includes any unskilful and compulsive thought pattern. We do not have to consume things compulsively and unskilfully to be an addict. We can be addicted to unskilful thought patterns, leading us to experience certain feelings, communicate in certain ways or take some form of physical action. For example, somebody may reactively create certain thoughts that lead him or her to feel guilty whenever they are blamed for something regardless of whether it was their fault. This is an example of an addiction.

We can repeat the same thought patterns that are perceived as automatic or uncontrollable when experiencing certain emotions. For example, feelings of anxiety may trigger thoughts about a stressful past experience. Feelings of excitement may trigger fantasies about a pleasure we have experienced before or would like to experience in the future. The addiction may contain a process where we see something, experience a feeling, run some habitual thought patterns and then act on those through reactive speech or physical action. These are complex processes playing out in our minds that connect what is coming in through the senses, bodily sensations, feelings, thoughts, speech and physical action.

When a particular cycle of addiction is in progress, we will always be lost in thought. An addiction is a pattern that is created within and connected with the past. This connection to the past may manifest visibly such as experiencing conscious thoughts or it could be operating at a deeper subconscious level without our awareness. Either way, the addiction is rooted in reactive conditioning from the past rather than responding skilfully to the present. Addictions and Presence cannot coexist as addictions need the realm of time to operate and Presence is timeless. In his book *The Power of Now* [10] Tolle associates addictions with pain describing how they always start with pain and end with pain. Addictions are established by the ego to escape from facing into emotional pain. Instead of allowing the pain to be released the ego stores it in an attempt to increase its size and dominance. Emotional pain is a core part of the ego.

At times, addictions in their current form may not be strong enough to escape from the pain, causing them to change shape or escalate. Addictions are like intelligent, but harmful viruses that morph and change to stay alive. If we take an addiction to alcohol as an example, the alcohol may lose its potency the more a person is used to consuming it. The addiction to alcohol can then escalate through increasing the drinking or to taking a different intoxicating substance in an attempt to escape from the underlying pain. Mental suffering can be triggered by feelings of shame that we experience after we have undertaken a particular sequence of addictive thoughts or behaviours. The suffering created from the shame is a helpful teacher and when it is viewed in that way, it can motivate us to change for the better. Although suffering is unpleasant and should be avoided wherever possible, it should never be judged as bad because it helps us to learn.

Gaining freedom from addictions allows creativity to flow freely. It is impossible for the mind to respond creatively to situations when it is reacting to habitual patterns, which is what happens during an active addiction cycle. At times when we are Present and free from addiction, the mind can respond wisely, based upon the conditions and knowledge we have at our disposal without being constrained by any preconceived impulse about how we should react. When addictions are released and creativity is allowed to flow, people are surprised at how skilfully they can respond to situations.

How Addictions Are Created

Addictions can be created at any time and are installed by the mind as an antidote to fear or pain. Take an example of a young child who is unable to deal with or escape from abusive parents. The child may create an escape route through an addiction. Escape may not be physically possible, so a mental escape route will be formed. This is initially perceived as providing freedom when in fact it is a bridge for true freedom to be gained at a later stage once the individual is ready. All addictions provide a temporary escape from pain in this way. In this example, the addiction may take all sorts of forms, but for now, let us assume the child escapes from pain caused by abusive parents by playing loud music. The music temporarily intoxicates the child and audibly distracts them from their difficult thoughts about the abuse. The addiction is then installed and the pattern repeated many times, creating a habit. Until the addiction is released, which may be years later, the same person, as an adult, may use loud music as an escape route from pain.

Many addictions are created at a young age through conditions created by unconscious parents and these can be some of the most challenging to release. When I walk around in public places, I observe many children with addictions to sugar. They are consuming far more sugar than their small bodies actually need. You may have witnessed the installation of this addiction through observing parents and their young children. You see a small child crying because they are bored or upset when they are out and about doing things with their parents, which the child has no interest in or need for. Their parents respond by giving the child some sweets or a biscuit. It is an easy option for the parents and harmful for the child. The parents who are taking a lead role in this process are often the only people who can change the situation. Many of these parents will not understand the impact of their actions. The association between pain and sugary food is then installed and ingrained in the mind of the child. If the addiction is not released, it continues into adulthood with comfort eating. Unfortunately, young children do not have the capacity to deal with this situation skilfully and have no choice but to accept the addiction. They carry it into adulthood with the possibility that they may be able to release it later in life if suffering or some other teachings wake them up to what they have inherited from their parents.

The creation and activation of addictions are governed by the ego when we are lost in thought. As we go about our daily activities, if we are lost in thought, we run the risk of new addictions being installed. The ego is very sneaky and does this whilst we are unaware. The installation is made deep in the subconscious mind where it may not even be detected. This explains why addictions and being lost in thought are so closely related. When you are Present, you are guarded against the installation of new addictions and triggering of existing addictions.

Addictions create thought, which is governed by the ego. The amount of time we are lost in thought is a factor of the number of addictions we have and the level of their intensity. If we have fewer addictions with lower intensity, our minds are far quieter and peaceful. The thoughts that are created by addictive patterns also trigger difficult emotions which impact the body and may drain our energy. All of this unnecessary thought leads to a lack of concentration, blocks creativity and leads us to unskilful action. The unskilful action then creates suffering, which triggers more addictions. This is a destructive and harmful cycle that we need to break by learning how to gain freedom from our addictions.

Gaining Freedom from Addictions

The first step in responding to an addiction is when we become aware that we have that addiction. The awareness may come through reflection after the addictive thoughts or behaviours, through experiencing feelings of shame or through somebody bringing the addiction to our attention. Once we are aware of the addiction, we then need to fully accept it. Thinking that it should not be there, blaming people who may have had a part in its creation or resisting it in any other way will feed the addiction and prevent its release. Once we have accepted the addiction, we will then be in a position to take positive action to gain freedom from it.

I once read a definition of an addiction being something that you can only be free of by utilizing external support. I cannot recall where I read this helpful definition. My extended interpretation of external support is that it represents support that is external to our own ego. This means that the support can be channelled through Presence. The guidance and courage to deal with the addiction may come from our own inner wisdom and resources, from somebody else guiding us or an external source such as a book or website. Presence is required to access wisdom that appears to come from within and to be receptive to another person or source. This implies that Presence is the antidote to all our addictions.

Once we are aware of the addiction and have brought acceptance to it, there are two approaches we can take to regain our freedom. The first is to manage our conditions to reduce or remove the possibility that the addiction is triggered. So somebody who has an addiction to chocolate may make a conscious effort to remove all chocolate from their home, thus reducing the probability that they will consume it there. If the addiction is an intoxicating thought fantasy, then we can bring awareness of thoughts or stimuli coming in through the senses that usually precede the fantasy and use them as triggers to regain Presence. So the objective here is to intervene through creating the right conditions and initiating Presence as early as possible in the addiction cycle. When I was addicted to caffeine and very aware, I could catch my subconscious mind planning when and how I would be having my next coffee. The addiction was running very subtle thought patterns that appeared quiet and distant like a dream. These thought patterns were then governing my future actions and reinforcing the addiction.

I remember supporting a friend who was working through alcohol and drug issues. I told her about the option of attending a local addictions clinic. In her initial consultation, she met with a recovering addict and told him about how she was going out to pubs and clubs with friends who drink and take drugs. She tried to stay sober during these times, but when she was out, she often found herself indulging. The recovering addict told her, "If you keep going back to the barber's, you'll eventually get your hair cut", which I felt was a wise response. Somebody else I knew said something similar: "If you're going to play rugby, be prepared to get dirty."

We must fully experience and accept the emotional pain that lies beneath an addiction in order to release it. When we are ready, conditions are presented to us that make this process easier. Let us take an example of somebody who is addicted to watching TV. They are at home one evening, the TV stops working and there is no other TV in their home to watch. The absence of watching TV then causes their emotional pain underneath the addiction to surface. If that person experiences the emotional pain fully and allows it to pass, they will heal, weaken or even release their addiction. The easier option here would be to use another distraction or addiction and dodge the emotional pain. The practice is to experience, accept and heal the emotional pain. Fortunately, our mind will only allow us to do this when we are ready and capable. Addictions act as temporary mechanisms to help us escape from the pain until we are ready to heal. This is why we carry addictions until we have the capacity to release them.

Addictions may be triggered by unpleasant feelings such as fear and stress. To create the right conditions, we must learn how to deal with those feelings skilfully. For example, somebody may drink alcohol if they are feeling socially anxious. A more suitable alternative would be to do some work outside of the situation to understand social anxiety. After reflecting, speaking with a friend or therapist, it may be wise to avoid that particular social situation altogether or if the person needs to return to it, they could learn some tactics that can be deployed at the time of experiencing the anxiety, which would give them more confidence and help to release the alcohol addiction. Tactics have their place, but ultimately we must face and work on the root cause of our addictions, which is always the underlying emotional pain.

The second approach to gaining freedom from addictions is to intervene when the addictive thought pattern, associated feelings or behaviours are activated. This is more challenging than the first option as the addictions increase in power once they are activated. The cycle builds momentum like a wave coming onto the shore before it crashes and then dissipates. Of course, with addictions, further waves follow until we gain freedom from them. So if we are inside the thought or behavioural pattern, our challenge is to interrupt it and break the cycle. This will only be possible if there is enough Presence available for us to realize that what we are doing is harmful, and the more awareness we bring to the addiction, the greater the chance of releasing it.

If we are aware of the addictive thought patterns, associated feelings or behaviours whilst they are in flow, the cycle can be stopped with assertive and significant action. The significance of the action must match the intensity of the thought pattern or behaviour in order to break out of the addictive cycle. So with a chocolate addiction, when you are eating chocolate, you may need to do something significant such as throwing it in the trash so that it cannot be consumed. With a thought fantasy, you may need to switch your attention to a positive and constructive activity that requires thought, which may mean physically moving or changing location in order to break state and force the change. Every time you intervene and interrupt addictive thought patterns or behaviours, you regain Presence, take right action, increase confidence and weaken the addiction.

Intervening with Presence when you experience unpleasant feelings *before* they generate unskilful thoughts is ideal. Many of the unpleasant feelings we experience cannot be prevented consciously as they are triggered by the subconscious mind. The best we can do in these cases is to bring awareness and acceptance to them. What is within our gift is to consciously let go of thoughts and stories that we tell ourself as a result of the feelings. It is these thoughts that are responsible for triggering further addictive actions and more unpleasant feelings. Our practice in these cases is to experience the feelings with full acceptance, let them go and return to the present moment. If we are aware of the thoughts and stories in our minds, we do the same with them. We bring awareness to them and allow them to pass.

Ideally, we would like to be totally free from the unskilful actions triggered by our addictions. If this is not possible, then giving our attention to the difficult feelings and thoughts for a short while before acting on the addiction will help. For example, if somebody is addicted to alcohol, ideally they will not take an alcoholic drink. But even if they did, if they sat with the craving and associated feelings for a while beforehand and gave them their full attention, that would enable some healing to take place and help to weaken the addiction. We often need to take small steps in the right direction before arriving at our goal. Every time we are aware of our emotional pain without escaping from it, even for short periods of time, we are healing ourself and evidencing progress which is empowering. If we are Present with others in pain, we are healing them. This is the practice of a true healer. They create Presence to allow others to release their emotional pain. The whole process of releasing addictions is a form of healing.

If you are at the stage where you can enable a state of Presence, you can use this as an intervention. In fact, it is the most effective intervention of them all. A gateway into this is concentration. You place all your concentration onto whatever object has been manifested by the addiction, including unpleasant thoughts, feelings and bodily sensations until they pass. It is common for people to sometimes uncover the root cause of the addiction when they are aware of the underlying emotional pain. A state of Presence helps us to see very deeply into our thought patterns, reactive feelings and memories. Understanding when and how our addictions were created may be interesting and helpful, but it is not strictly a prerequisite for releasing them.

Cravings manifested through our addictions are a form of energy. The source of the craving is the ego and when we are Present, we can reclaim that energy. When we meet cravings with Presence and allow them to pass, the energy can be used skilfully and positively. When I practise this, I liken myself to a phone that has been plugged into the mains and charged up. I can literally feel the energy building within me. As a consequence, we can diminish the ego's energy and power, thus reducing it. If we can work through an addictive craving in this way and stay aware of the body, we will literally feel the energy moving around within us. When we act out of an addiction, the energy is released unskilfully. Addictions consume a lot of energy and can be tiring due to their high emotional content and the suffering that follows. This is why people who are more Present enjoy a much higher balance of consistent energy compared to people with significant addictions whose energy will rise and crash as they go through their addictive cycles.

The two approaches, which are managing conditions and intervening with Presence can be used together. For example, smokers may change their conditions by removing themselves from the company of other smokers or taking nicotine substitutes, but this may not be enough to prevent them from smoking. They will also need to intervene with Presence when they experience cravings. Working on the conditions is a proactive approach and intervening with Presence is a responsive tactic.

It may not be possible for us to gain freedom from certain addictions on our own, implying that we need support from others including friends, therapists or specialist support organizations. This support may be available in the form of resources such as books, websites or products that can be used to help release the addiction. Once we access support, it means that we have accepted that we have the addiction or that there is the possibility that we have it, which is the first step. We need to access the right type of support to suit our character and situation. This may involve doing some research and taking different routes before we find the right support option or combination of options to move forward. I know from experience that getting support can be a difficult step for those who may not be used to asking others for help or have grown up in a culture believing that people should be self-sufficient and deal with their own problems. I have seen therapists on a number of occasions, which helped with my own addictions and have friends who have done the same.

Addictions are not part of our true essence, which shines through when we are Present. Our past conditioning cannot be changed and we do not consciously plan to create addictions. Addictions are created out of ignorance and because we were lost in thought. Accepting the past is wise and resisting it causes suffering. It is futile to resist what has already happened. Our opportunity to change and become more conscious human beings always lies within the present moment.

It is inevitable that from time to time we will follow our addictive patterns and if we are receptive, we will experience feelings of shame. This is part of the learning cycle and the mind's way of teaching us through feelings. Our job is then to regain Presence, reflect on our actions and accept what has happened, which leads to self-forgiveness. We can resolve any problems that we have caused through our actions if it is possible and appropriate for us to do so. We then go on to make whatever changes can be made to our current or future conditions and continue working on gaining freedom from the addiction. Our job of working with addictions will last until we are fully awakened and constantly Present. Until that point we will always be conditioned by the past to some extent. Addictions are always created when we are lost in thought. They can never be created from a mind that is Present, which makes Presence the only real antidote. To increase our motivation to release an addiction, we should spend time reflecting on the adverse consequences, the risk it is introducing in our life, and the harm it is causing to ourself and others.

There is always a timing consideration when releasing addictions. We have to be both motivated and capable of releasing them. This explains why people experience a tension between wanting to release an addiction and not wanting to release an addiction. A few years ago, I remember having regular discussions with an alcoholic. This man faced the same dilemma that is faced by many during the lifetime of an addiction. He wanted to stop drinking but also wanted to continue drinking. His true essence was wise and knew that he needed to stop. The problem was that his ego that was identified with the addiction wanted him to continue. As a person evolves spiritually, the connection with their true self increases and their ego reduces. During this period of tension, the individual can be supported through pointers to their true self by way of spiritual teachings or more specialist support to help release addictions. Once the connection with their true self is strong enough, they will pass over a tipping point and find themselves in a confident position to release the addiction.

There is truth in the phrase "they will do it when they are ready". For the fortunate, this process runs its course and the addiction is released. Sadly, for others, the addiction remains and creates a lot of suffering, but the tipping point is never reached within their lifetime. They then die due to the addiction or some other factor with the addictive thought patterns still intact at the time of death. I keep an open mind about what happens when one dies and have no opinion on the subject of re-birth and the transferring of karma from one life to the next. I do not understand how or if this takes place and nor do I need to. What I know for sure is that at the time of death, I want my mind to be pure and free from any unhelpful past conditioning that causes suffering. I also know that the more we all work towards this vision within our lifetimes, the happier and peaceful the human race will be.

The World's Biggest Addiction

Within his Internet subscription service Eckhart Tolle Now [11], Eckhart suggests that thinking may be the biggest addiction that faces the human race. Personally, I believe this to be true. The biggest addiction people face is the addiction to thought. It is only through becoming aware of our habitual thoughts are we able to acknowledge and take responsibility for them. Even addictions that appear to be physical and action orientated will be thought generated, as actions are controlled by thoughts. All of our speech and every action are the result of either conscious or subconscious thought patterns. Even something as simple as walking is governed by the mind albeit subconsciously for the majority of the time.

We may believe that our addictions are related to thought patterns, feelings, speech, actions or a combination of all four. Examples may include an addiction to envious thoughts, an addiction to excitement, an addiction to swearing or an addiction to coughing. When we look closely at our so-called 'addiction' we can observe that it is non-existent as a fixed form. Where does it start and finish? Is the addiction the thought, feeling, speech or action? If it is the thought, which thought or thoughts is it exactly? Is it that particular thought pattern we are addicted to or the thought patterns leading up to it? Where exactly is the addiction? It is because there is no absolute reality of addictions that we can become free of them. We are not becoming free of the addiction, but free of the identification to the concept of the addiction. Thoughts are always involved with addictions and this is why Presence is required to gain freedom from them. A level of consciousness higher than thoughts is required.

To summarize, if we are ever lost in thought and unskilful, our ego, via the addictions it identifies with has taken the driving seat. Addictions are reactive and habitual. When we gain freedom from our addictions, even if only for a short period of time, we gain access to our true essence, which is peaceful, loving and creative. Presence protects us from old addictions being triggered and from the creation of new addictions. One could say that the spiritual life is all about gaining freedom from addictions and once they have all been released we are fully awakened.

Relating to Addictions

Our addictions should not be judged as bad, despite what we may hear from others, including the media. Judging anything as bad is unhelpful and ignorant because what we judge does not exist in any fixed form. It is impermanent. There is a difference between judging something as bad and judging something as unskilful. Accurately judging something as unskilful recognizes that we can see it is causing harm which is helpful. Judging something as bad means we are fundamentally disagreeing with how things are at a given point in time. Another way of expressing this is that we are in resistance to the present moment and what is. We can differentiate between these two forms of judgement by examining the feeling tones in our bodies at the time the judgement is made. 'Bad' judgements carry a negative energy and cause stress as judging things, situations and people as bad is actually a form of delusion. This is going into battle with the universe or God! We will lose every time.

The concept of an addiction circles around unique thought processes that arise and pass. The same goes for flowers in that we can label them as a type of flower, but every flower is different and constantly changing if we were to examine it closely enough. It can be helpful to label an addiction to help us conceptualize and think critically about it, but the truth is that nothing is really fixed or can be pinned down in any shape or form. So we can go ahead and think or talk about addictions whilst keeping in mind that the word 'addiction' is merely a concept and the thought patterns that the concept points to are subject to change. It is this change and fluidity that allows us to be creative, let go of old conditioning and move in a more conscious direction. The whole process of our experience is fluid and continuously changing. Our minds label things and assume they are fixed and exist in their own right to try and make sense of the world.

When we are reflecting on our addictions and working to gain freedom from them, we should develop an attitude of friendly curiosity. Addictions are installed by the ego so that we can escape from pain. To help let go of judging our addictions, we can remind ourself that they have a positive intention to move us away from pain, but are helping us in an inappropriate way. Acknowledging this makes it easier to meet them with friendliness. We can relate to addictions positively in the same way that we can relate to a good friend who is trying their best to help, but is actually causing us problems in the process. We can be curious about what the addiction is looking to achieve and to bring awareness to the underlying pain that triggered its creation.

It is not always easy to admit that we have an addiction, because of stigma, guilt or fear about how others might judge us. If we do choose to reveal our addictions to others, we should ask ourself whether the person we are revealing them to is capable of listening carefully, discreetly and without judgement. Also, if we do reveal an addiction to others, there may be an indirect expectation that they will be able to hold the confidential and sensitive information. Again, we should ask ourself whether it is reasonable to expect them to do this for us. Ideally, at the time of sharing details about an addiction, the person whom you are sharing with should be Present. Similarly, when reflecting or working on addictions in solitude then do so with Presence. With Presence enabled, the response to the addiction will come from a place of acceptance and love, placing you in an ideal position to transcend it.

Addictions Attracting Addictions

I find it helpful to learn about addictions by observing them operating. In doing this, I have noticed that people attract other people who have the same addiction. For example, this is common in the case of alcohol and drug addiction. Many years ago I was in a relationship with a woman who was working to let go of a recreational drug addiction. She told me that wherever she travelled, she would automatically attract and connect with other drug users without any conscious effort. When we are lost in thought, addictions are intelligent enough to seek out any opportunity to manifest, including places, situations and other people. It is largely a subconscious process that happens in the background of our thoughts and a great deal of awareness is required to notice it happening within us. More subtle addictions, such as complaining about situations, operate in the same way. This is why people often come together to complain. People also connect with each other and build rapport by fantasizing together about the things they are addicted to.

It may help to make a conscious effort to remove ourself from the company of others who share our addictions. This provides us with space to heal the underlying pain and reduces the chances of the addiction being triggered. Every time addictive actions are triggered, they are reinforced. Therefore, the more space we create between the triggers, the better. The more infrequent the triggers, the more our addictions weaken and lose their power over us. This method of working with our addictions can be challenging as it may mean letting go of other benefits in our relationship with others. With drug addiction, a group of people who take drugs together may also have positive needs met, such as companionship and fun. If one parts company with that group, they may miss the positive aspects of the contact and will need to create new friends so that their needs can be met in a more nourishing way. It can sometimes be possible to maintain our relationships with others by avoiding places or situations where the addictions will get triggered and replacing them with something more nourishing. A great example of this is a well-run support group for addicts. These environments and organizations are proven to be highly beneficial for many and worth considering as an aid to release an addiction.

Finally, I would like to point out that releasing certain addictions might require support from specialist medical professionals and therapists. More serious addictions to alcohol and drugs may even cause life threatening seizures. In these extreme cases carefully prescribed medical interventions will be required. If in doubt, always consult your doctor for advice on addictions in the first instance.

POINTS FOR REFLECTION

- Addictions are unskilful, compulsive thought patterns that can only be released through Presence.

- Understanding addictions and taking responsibility to release them is an essential part of spiritual practice.

- We are not the same person from one moment to the next and with that knowledge we can be empowered to make positive changes and release our addictions.

- An addiction is rooted in reactive conditioning from the past rather than responding to what is appropriate in the present.

- Addictions and Presence cannot coexist as addictions need the realm of time to operate and Presence is timeless.

- Addictions can be created at any time and are installed by the mind as an antidote to fear or pain.

- The creation and activation of addictions are governed by the ego when we are lost in thought.

- We must fully experience and accept the emotional pain that lies beneath an addiction to gain freedom from it.

- Every time we are aware of our emotional pain without escaping from it, even for short periods of time, we are healing ourself and evidencing progress which is empowering.

- Addictions are like intelligent, but harmful viruses that morph and change to stay alive.

- Gaining freedom from addictions allows creativity to flow freely.

- When we are Present, we are guarded against new addictions being installed and existing addictions being triggered.

- Presence is the antidote to all our addictions.

- To increase our motivation to release an addiction, we can spend time reflecting on the adverse consequences, the risk it is introducing into our life, and the harm it is causing to ourself or others.

- Our minds will only allow us to work on addictions when we are ready and capable. This is why we carry addictions until we have the capacity to release them.

- It may not be possible for us to gain freedom from certain addictions on our own.

- The biggest addiction people face is the addiction to thought.

- Acceptance is an essential step when working to release addictions.

- People may attract other people who have the same addiction.

- When we are lost in thought, addictions are intelligent enough to seek out any opportunity to manifest, including places, situations and other people.

- Although suffering is unpleasant and should be avoided wherever possible, it should never be viewed as bad because it helps us to learn.

- It may help to make a conscious effort to remove ourself from the company of others who share our addictions.

- Well-run support groups for addicts are proven to be highly beneficial for many and worth considering as an aid to release certain addictions.

- Releasing certain addictions may require support from specialist medical professionals and therapists. If in doubt, always consult your doctor for advice.

- One could say that the spiritual life is all about gaining freedom from addictions and once they have all been released, we are fully awakened.

OPTIONAL LEARNING ACTIVITIES

- List your addictions and prioritize them for releasing. For each addiction, make a note of

  (i)   when you think it may have been created

  (ii) how it is triggered

  (iii) the actions that it triggers

  (iv) the consequences of those actions and

  (v) the next steps in releasing it.

  Remember to include addictive thought patterns in this list.
  Select one or two addictions that you would like to start work on.

- To increase your motivation to release an addiction, spend time reflecting on the adverse consequences, the risk it is introducing in your life and the harm it is causing to yourself or others.

- If you have a meditation practice, keep a note of any addictive thought patterns that arise during your meditation sessions.

- Keep an addiction journal. When you experience cravings related to addictions or if you react to the addiction through speech or physical action, make an entry. Also, note the conditions that led up to the craving and action. Review your journal on a regular basis and see if you can identify themes.

- Get into the habit of placing all your concentration onto whatever has been manifested by the addictive pattern, including unpleasant thoughts, feelings and bodily sensations until they pass.

- Consider getting some support. This may be through friends, therapy, information, products, services or groups.

Chapter Eight

Stillness, Spaciousness & Nature

A number of gateways into Presence have been introduced, including the breath, movement, body awareness, communication, and meditation. This chapter introduces a further three gateways that provide a range of opportunities to enter the present moment which are stillness, spaciousness, and nature.

Stillness of the Body

When the body is still, emotions and thoughts naturally follow. If we stay in a still position for long enough whilst remaining alert and relaxed, this will help us to become Present. This may happen in a few seconds or could take hours, depending on the conditions leading up to the physical stillness. Personally, if I am relatively calm and relaxed, then I can achieve a state of Presence in a number of seconds or minutes. If I have been lost in thought for most of the day and feeling emotional, then it could take an hour or longer of physical stillness before the mind becomes quiet.

We can create opportunities to become still. Even if we are not fully Present, stillness will allow us to become more mindful and aware of our thoughts, feelings and bodily sensations. It helps if we can temporarily disengage with any thought-generating activity, such as watching TV, reading or using our phone during the practice. We simply sit or stand very still and wait patiently for the Presence to arise within us. This stillness practice is a form of meditation and is flexible enough to be introduced in most environments for anything from a few seconds to hours at a time. Using this practice before sleep and upon waking will increase sleep quality and help start our day with Presence. It can also be practised in public places such as when we are waiting in a queue.

Stillness enables us to work with our feelings. With most feelings, even the unpleasant ones, if we observe them diligently, they will pass within a couple of minutes. For example, when we are feeling anxious, we can locate the anxiety in our bodies and observe how it is manifesting. If we are fully aware of the anxiety, then our mind will remain quiet without judging it or creating stories. To begin with, it can be helpful for us to use labels such as excitement, depression, fear, peace, happiness and so on to establish a conceptual connection with our feelings. As we become more advanced with this practice, we can let go of labelling our feelings with specific names. Instead, we can label them as pleasant, unpleasant or neutral.

When we look closely, we notice that feelings are unique in terms of their form and movement. We can experience them directly and let go of feeding them with unnecessary judgements and thoughts. This erodes part of the ego and helps us to gain freedom and peace from these types of feelings in the future. It sets us up to respond creatively in the present moment rather than producing and reacting to historical feelings that are no longer relevant.

The stillness practice teaches us about impermanence. We may realize at an intellectual level that all form (including ourself) is transient and nothing is ultimately fixed. By bringing awareness to our direct experience, we begin to understand this at a much deeper level. The deeper we understand this, the less we get blown around when things change in situations where we have a preference for them to stay as they are. This can apply to literally anything, ranging from a household appliance breaking down, the death of a loved one or a long-term relationship with our partner ending. A deeper understanding of impermanence cultivates equanimity, which is our ability to stay grounded and skilful amidst chaotic and challenging situations.

Our understanding of impermanence may be deepened through a significant life event such as a serious illness, loss of a loved one or even significant personal gain. Regardless of whether we embark on a practice of Presence or connect with spiritual teachings, the universe will naturally teach us about impermanence. Even when we are not consciously working on becoming more Present, our conditions automatically provide the opportunities for us to learn and progress.

Two events relating to impermanence that everybody experiences are birth and death. Although death is something we can absolutely count on, most of us do relatively little to prepare for it. Understanding impermanence and becoming more Present allows us to experience illness and ultimately to let go of our bodies peacefully when it is natural to do so. This then reduces the greatest fear of all for most of us, which is the fear of death. Presence creates a more confident and peaceful existence in the relatively short time we inhabit the earth.

Space between Objects

The third stage of Presence Meditation discussed in Chapter Four provides a technique for becoming Present through bringing our awareness to the space in-between form. This technique can also be used outside of meditation. Form includes everything we are aware of. Thoughts, feelings, bodily sensations and things entering the senses are all part of form. When we have a moment whilst sitting or standing, we can practise this by investigating the space between the physical objects that surround us. For example, if we are seated on a bench and there are trees around us, we can explore the space in-between ourself and the trees. When we are seated at a desk using our computer, we can explore the space between ourself and the computer. There is nothing in particular to look at, just empty space. Space is free from all physical characteristics, making it impossible to label or judge, which helps to calm the mind.

Exploring space in this way leads us into Presence. I often pause to do this if I am involved in an activity such as writing. When I feel tired, I stop and explore the space around me for a few seconds. This is enough to refresh me, clear my mind, enable Presence and allow that to flow into the writing when I continue. Taking pauses in this way aligns to the natural cycle of work and rest that can be observed in any balanced activity and in nature. I do the same if I am stationary in traffic. I explore the space within my car or the space between my car and other cars. This technique provides a break from form, which is what we are usually focused on.

Silence

Exploring space between form includes exploring silence. Most environments are not silent. Even in a quiet room, we may hear subtle sounds such as a clock ticking or the sound of our own breath. If we listen carefully, we can find pockets of silence between the sounds. If the sounds are continuous, such as the humming of an air conditioning unit, we can pay attention to the silence around them.

Every sound we hear has silence around it. When we are paying attention to silence, we are paying attention to nothing. Silence is empty. It is through this emptiness that we can enter a state of Presence. We may also use the pockets of silence in our communication as part of this practice. When we are listening to people, we can pay attention to the silence between the words or the silence when they have finished speaking. If we have finished a conversation with somebody, we can give our attention to the subsequent space and silence for a few seconds before moving on to our next activity.

There are opportunities everywhere to give our attention to silence. When I use my laptop keyboard, I occasionally take the opportunity to place my attention on the silence in-between the key taps. Our breath contains brief pockets of silence at the end of the in-breath or the out-breath. When a car engine or house alarm stops, you can give your attention to the space or silence that is perceived. I have suffered from tinnitus for most of my adult life. I continuously hear a very high-pitched sound. Even with this condition, it is still possible to give my attention to silence as the silence surrounds the high-pitched sound. This provides freedom from the condition in the same way that observing the space around physical pain allows us to be the awareness observing it rather than the pain itself.

Space between Hindrances

In Chapter Five, a number of internal hindrances are introduced: Sensory desire, ill will, sloth and torpor, restlessness and worry, and doubt. They may be experienced through the ego feeding off worldly conditions. There may be certain times when the hindrances constitute the bulk of our experience. This is more likely to be within situations that we find challenging.

I recall these hindrances playing a big part in my experiences during business conferences at work. These were often multi-day events where anything up to one hundred people would attend. I would take on the role as presenter or facilitator for part of the event. I would be expected to network and also take on board a vast amount of information that was being presented by others. I was outside of my comfort zone. My personality is introverted. I usually influence my own working conditions to create an abundance of silence, solitude, space and breaks from thought, which suits me and provides an environment to be productive and creative. As you might imagine, the contrast I experienced at these conferences was significant and remaining Present was a real challenge. The ego had a wonderful time. During the conferences, I would experience every type of hindrance a number of times. This would include worrying about my presentation going wrong, feeling anxious about how I might be judged by others, craving to be alone, craving silence, experiencing ill will towards the odd person there who I did not like and doubting whether I was in the right job[12].

I never expected to be fully Present throughout the conferences. That felt like too much to ask, given the challenges I faced. Gradually, as I worked more on my practice, I started to notice gaps of thought opening up. To begin with, they only lasted a few seconds. With each conference, the gaps became more frequent and longer in duration. Even in that busy environment, ninety-nine percent of the time there was no real need to think. The bulk of my thoughts were related to the hindrances. So these conferences became beneficial to my practice. They provided a working ground. A calling to temporarily let go of controlling my environment, surrender to the experience whilst I was there and become more Present. Because they were held every few months, they became a benchmarking opportunity where I could measure my Presence increasing. If I made progress, including a relatively small amount, from one conference to the next, I was grateful.

The learning point here is that we can always reframe a difficult situation into a positive opportunity. If we look closely enough at our experience during these times, we find pockets of spaciousness and peace between the hindrances. They may appear small and infrequent to begin with and as we evolve, they permeate more of our experience. As a practice, we can look out for these pockets of spaciousness in our planned and spontaneous meditation. Regularly cultivating this gateway into Presence during meditation creates a habit to do the same outside of meditation.

Sleep

Bringing awareness to our physical experience when we are lying in bed at night before sleep and when we wake up in the morning allows us to enter into sleep through Presence and start the day with Presence. Many of us may find that without any conscious effort the opposite is true, which is that we are lost in thought when we fall to sleep and spend the first few moments of each day lost in thought. Becoming aware at these times is a practice that can take time to cultivate if we need to change old habits. Small progressive steps are helpful and the process itself, in my opinion, regardless of the outcome, is thoroughly enjoyable and positively transforms our experience of falling to sleep and waking up.

With this practice, we are introducing two short planned meditations into every day. Everything else being equal, if we enter sleep through Presence, our sleep quality and the amount of deep sleep we experience will increase. It is also a pleasant way of entering sleep and is far more helpful than experiencing thoughts based upon the hindrances such as anxiety or craving. The morning practice helps get our day off to a good start as we are setting the tone with awareness and consciousness. We can also integrate this practice into any naps that we take throughout the day, which will open up further meditation opportunities.

Nature

A gateway for Presence that is readily accessible to us all is nature. What do we mean by nature? In the context of Presence and to provide a definition for use within this book, we can assume nature to be any form that has been created naturally. This could be a flower, a tree, the sky, the ocean, a droplet of water etc. It also includes seeing the nature within a human creation. If we look closely at a wooden table, we will see the wood grain that originated from the tree from which the table was made. We can also find nature in people, animals and insects.

To gain Presence through nature, we must experience it without labelling. When we are looking, hearing, smelling or feeling nature, the intention should be awareness of our direct experience. When we label our experience, this involves thoughts, judgements or cravings which dilutes the experience. For example, we may see a dog and say to ourself, "That is a friendly dog. I have not seen a dog like that before. I am curious as to what type of dog it is. It looks a little similar to the dog I spotted the other week when I was with my friend. Maybe I should get in touch with my friend and arrange to meet again… etc… etc…" Before we know it, we are lost in thought. We may even call or message our friend immediately to share the news and in the meantime, the opportunity to continue to experience the beauty of the dog passes us by. We miss the present moment through being lost in the past and future. Our knowledge can hinder us in these situations as the more knowledge we have, the easier it can be for our mind to make connections with what we directly experience or filter the experience out altogether.

If we are knowledgeable about the sea, this can make it difficult for us to experience it directly without some mental commentary on the reasons for the size of the waves, temperature, colour and other characteristics. People who share what they know when they are in familiar environments or situations sometimes display this. It is wonderful to share knowledge consciously when we are Present, but when shared unconsciously it can give the mind an opportunity to escape from what is taking place for us now. It also provides the ego with an opportunity to strengthen through demonstrating knowledge regardless of whether it is useful for the recipients. We must make even more of an effort to stay Present in surroundings and areas in which we are knowledgeable.

When we have an opportunity to observe nature, we can make a conscious effort to observe it directly for a period of time. This can be an uncomfortable practice to start with because we are surrendering to the moment and allowing it to connect us with something that is very vast and mysterious. Despite this being so wonderful and deep, it can be difficult to contain as our ego or the false sense of self will feel threatened and do its best to pull us back into self-referential thought to confirm that we exist as a fixed entity. This is delusional and causes us to suffer. The same thing can be experienced within our meditation if we become deeply Present. Being attentive to nature that does not involve humans is a good place to start. For most of us, when we observe people, there is more of a tendency to label and judge them. This is less likely with a flower, animal, tree, cloud or some other natural object of the non-human kind. As we progress, we become more skilled at this and we then find it easier to place our attention onto people and be free from any discursive thought.

The time taken for nature to lead us into Presence varies based upon our state of consciousness at the time. When our mind becomes still and we experience peace or joy, we know that we are Present. When we go out into a natural setting we might spend much of the time talking to ourself in our minds about the past or future. Couples or groups of people do the same. They are walking in a beautiful environment, which is longing for their attention. Instead of surrendering to it, they spend the whole time 'catching up' and talking about what has happened in their lives over the last few weeks and what they have planned. Reflecting and planning have their place and are helpful as long as they are performed consciously. So if we are taking a walk in nature with the conscious intention of talking about the past or future, that will work well and prove beneficial. However, if we are doing this in an addictive or habitual fashion, then we will be lost in thought and feeding the ego.

POINTS FOR REFLECTION

- When the body becomes still our emotions and thoughts naturally follow.

- With most feelings, even the unpleasant ones, if we observe them diligently they will pass within a couple of minutes.

- We can neutralize feelings through experiencing them directly and by letting go of feeding them with unnecessary thoughts and judgements.

- A deeper understanding of impermanence cultivates equanimity, which is our ability to stay grounded and skilful amidst chaotic and challenging situations.

- We can always reframe a difficult situation into a positive opportunity.

- Bringing awareness to our physical experience when we are lying in bed at night before sleep and when we wake up in the morning allows us to enter into sleep through Presence and start the day with Presence.

- Nature is a gateway into Presence that is readily accessible to us all.

- To gain Presence through nature we must experience it without labelling.

OPTIONAL LEARNING ACTIVITIES

- Take opportunities to explore the space in and around form for a few seconds within your day-to-day activities.

- Pay attention to the silence around sounds.

- When you are listening to others, pay attention to the silence between their words or the silence when they have finished speaking.

- Bring awareness to your physical experience when lying in bed at night before sleep and when you wake up in the morning.

- Practise keeping the body still for periods of time and observe how your thoughts and feelings will naturally become less frequent.

- Review and play with the frequency of your contact with nature and observe how this helps with your practice.

Chapter Nine

Acceptance

When we fully accept things as they are, including thoughts, feelings, bodily sensations and external situations, we are free from suffering. The more we reflect upon this, the more motivated we will be to greet our experience with acceptance. The more effective we become at greeting our experience with acceptance, the more we will trust that things are the way they are and were always going to end up that way. Through acceptance, our level of fear reduces and we can enjoy a real sense of confidence, lightness and freedom. Thoughts do not need to be judged, controlled or pushed away and should never be viewed as bad or wrong. If we tell ourself that we should not think what we have just thought, we need to understand that all our thoughts happen for a reason and they can never be changed once they have manifested. Presence allows them to be acknowledged and to pass with a conscious decision as to whether they should be followed up.

Acceptance does not mean living passively without making any changes to improve our situation. Acceptance is a real-time practice that relates to our experience in the present moment. If we are aware of being in pain or suffering, then we should take action to avoid the same happening in the future if we can. For example, if we experience a headache, we first accept the physical pain. Mentally, we might say, "I have an uncomfortable pain in my head and that is how it is right now." No resistance or complaining is required as this will create psychological suffering and may extend or increase the pain. From there, we can reflect on what may have caused the headache or what we can do to reduce or remove it. The intention must always be to accept what is happening in the present moment and take action when required to positively influence the future. How do we know what action is required? This enters our awareness spontaneously through Presence.

Through acceptance, we become peaceful, aligned with the present moment and in touch with who we really are. It transports us to ultimate freedom regardless of the situation we find ourself in. Out of acceptance comes the freedom to take skilful action. Acceptance aligns us with exactly how things are now, which puts us in the best possible place to access our inner wisdom and respond creatively to whatever is required. This is not the wisdom from the thinking mind or our ego, but a transcendental intelligence that is connected with and considers everything.

If we are not in a state of acceptance, we are in a state of resistance. This includes resistance to situations such as waiting in a queue of traffic, a comment we find difficult or a feeling of embarrassment as food misses our mouth and hits our shirt over dinner. It also includes resistance to something more immediate such as a thought or feeling. The body reacts to resistance with tension and illness so through being more accepting, we significantly increase our chances of staying physically well. It is the ego that resists things. Our true essence is always accepting, as all things need to be accepted. Just as our true essence can be described as awareness or love, it also can be described as acceptance. Resisting anything we experience is pointless because whatever has been manifested has been manifested. Resisting something means that we are craving for the universe to be different to how it is now. The universe cannot possibly be different to how it is now. We cannot turn back the clock and change things. When we crave for things to be different, we suffer and this implies we are lost in thought. When we are lost in thought, we have lost touch with our true essence and acceptance. Being lost in thought creates more harm and suffering until the point at which we become Present again. This is the unpleasant cycle of resistance that we need to free ourself from. Many people believe that control as a reaction to resistance provides power. They are wrong. Acceptance and the present moment provide power.

How to Accept

How do we accept things? It is all very well and good for somebody to recommend that we be more accepting, but how is that possible? People might say, "You must be more accepting of the situation" or, "You must accept her." Acceptance is not possible through craving for things to be different now to how they are now. This is how we resist what is rather than accepting what is. If we let go of resistance, we will be in a state of acceptance and we let go of resistance by letting go of craving. Letting go of craving is a fundamental teaching from the Buddha. He explained that it is required to gain freedom from suffering in order to attain enlightenment. His teachings then provide a path that can be used as a guide to practice, including areas on wisdom, ethics and concentration. We will not go into the detail of the Buddha's guidance here, but it is true to say that working in these areas of practice will lead us to Presence. Paths like these are not exclusive to Buddhism. Teachings from other religions that are grounded in the truth of how things really are will lead us to the same destination.

Acceptance of how things are in the present allows us to be aligned with the flow of conditions. At the point of acceptance, we are fully aligned with everything that has happened in our experience beforehand and everything that may happen in the future. This has to be true as it is the only way that we can accept the present. The reverse is also true. If we are resisting the past or resisting the perceived future, we are resisting the present. This acceptance of the past and future triggered through acceptance of the present leads to peace. Presence is timeless and the past and the future are both infinite. Acceptance and Presence go together. Acceptance implies Presence. When you are in acceptance, you must be Present and when you are Present, you must be in acceptance of what is.

Working with Resistance

Acceptance is our natural state and it cannot be forced. When we are in touch with who we truly are, we will be in full acceptance of the present moment. Acceptance is our natural state of being and resistance blocks it. Resistance is due to craving for things to be different to how they are now and is always initiated by the ego. This can happen when we have our buttons pressed. We react to certain situations or people, causing us to judge them and crave for them or things to be different. Resistance pushes us out of the present moment and creates stress whereas acceptance keeps us within the present moment. If we become aware of certain situations leading to a state of resistance, we should investigate the causes and either bring acceptance to them or initiate changes.

Resistance is common in relationships, including friendships, personal relationships, professional relationships and family relationships. This is experienced when one person does something that triggers resistance in the other. In these cases, one of three things happen: (i) things remain as is and the suffering continues (ii) things change and the relationship improves or (iii) the relationship ends.

I have experienced this many times in personal relationships. Friends, family members and partners behaved in certain ways and I was unable to accept my reactions towards them. I resisted, judged them, became upset and expected them to be different to how they were. On every occasion one of three things happened. Either (i) I continued to suffer (ii) we made some adjustments to improve the relationship or (iii) we let go of the relationship altogether. Whatever the outcome, we must keep in mind that this is a natural process which does not need to be judged or forced. The process itself needs acceptance. I often judged myself for not being accepting enough in relationships, which simply added more resistance and suffering. My therapist once told me that it would be crazy to put my hand in a fire even if I could withstand it! That helped give me the confidence to change things. Sometimes people judge us for taking action to gain freedom from our resistance and that is fine. That is their resistance that they must work with. The truth is that our experiences of resistance and acceptance guide us through life and keep us on the path for which we are intended. This is the path to becoming more Present.

I recall a time many years ago when I used to spend five days each week in an office environment. For some people, this suited them just fine. For me, it was stressful. I was in resistance to this situation for a long time and continued without really understanding what was happening within me and suffering as a result. It was only later when my circumstances changed that I gained some perspective. A change in role allowed me to work from home for part of the week and I realized that I had a need for solitude that was not being met. At the time, my busy weekdays at work were spent with colleagues and customers. My weekends were spent with my family. I had not connected with the spiritual path at the time and knew nothing about acceptance and resistance. Like many people, I simply carried on resisting the same situation, becoming more and more stressed. Once I created the right balance, I felt at peace with my work and enjoyed being in the office on the days I was there. Since then, I have learned that if I am feeling resistance towards a situation, I should make an effort to explore it and understand what needs to change.

This practice of managing resistance is about taking responsibility for our life conditions and responding kindly to our own needs. We will only investigate areas of resistance when we are ready to do so. Through intervening and taking corrective action, the less we suffer, the less harm we cause and the more peaceful and happier we become. If we do not take responsibility for the changes, then at some point the universe will take care of things for us, but be warned, this may take some time and result in a great deal of suffering along the way. We should take responsibility for our own life conditions and change things when required. We need to be careful not to make changes too hastily. Sometimes resistance will pass naturally so this should be considered before making changes to situations. We can speak to wise friends, analyse the situation and draw upon our own experience and that of others before making decisions. This is especially relevant in the more significant areas of life such as livelihood, living situation, family and relationships.

Relative & Absolute Acceptance

Relatively speaking, the concept of time must be factored into acceptance. Let us take an example where we need to bring acceptance to a computer crashing and losing documents we have been working on. The acceptance required is not just about the computer crashing. It also includes accepting some of what may lead on from that. For example, the document may be required for a customer or submission to support an academic qualification with a deadline. So we may need to reset the deadline or work unsociable hours to recover the document. I label the broad acceptance of situations like this *relative acceptance* as it is based in the realm of time. Relative acceptance implies that we need to accept what has happened already or what may happen.

Relative acceptance is helpful as a concept, but it is actually an illusion created by the mind. It is not really possible to accept what has happened or what might happen. What has happened cannot be accepted now as it is in the past and what may happen is not there to accept yet. So the only real acceptance is acceptance of the present moment, which is *absolute acceptance*. We may conceptually believe that we have accepted something that has happened to us, but all we are really accepting is our experience (including thoughts and feelings) about it at a moment in time. It can feel as though we have accepted something in our past on one day and then become resistant to it again later. For example, we might accept something that a friend said that we found hurtful, but the following week we are back in resistance and judging them. This is because we are accepting or resisting our experience about a past situation at a future point in time. Our experience has the potential to change based on the preceding conditions. We cannot accept something that has already taken place in absolute terms. We can only ever accept our experience within the present moment.

Absolute acceptance means saying 'yes' to the present moment, 'yes' to what is.. It is a real-time, here-and-now practice requiring no complexity or consideration of time. This is a very simple form of acceptance, which happens automatically when we are Present. We simply accept everything that enters our awareness in any given moment. No looking backward or forward required, just a real-time acceptance of what is now. A thought pops into our head and we accept it. A feeling is experienced and we accept it. We become aware of a bodily sensation and we accept it. We are aware of form coming in through the senses and we accept it. This can be trained within a meditative context. When we are sitting in meditation, we will be practising awareness. As things come into our awareness, we can accept them. If we find ourself resisting what enters our awareness, the next job is to accept the fact that we are resisting. We accept the resistance. This can also be a practice outside of meditation. Practising absolute acceptance is about befriending our experience. This includes unpleasant feelings, thoughts and bodily sensations. These experiences need to be held gently and kindly in the same way we might hold a small animal that we are caring for. Part of our practice is to be the love around absolutely everything, including what we dislike or find unpleasant.

The more we can practise absolute acceptance, the less we need to practise relative acceptance. If we can accept our experience as it arises and stay Present, there is no need to accept anything within the realm of time as it will be accepted as a consequence. Time is simply a sequence of present moments. With this method, our life is much easier to navigate because we are aligned with our true self. This means we will understand exactly what situations require from us. Absolute acceptance requires no thought, effort or force. Only surrender.

We need to strike a balance between practising the two forms of acceptance. We can use relative acceptance to consciously think about how to work with resistance in situations and practise absolute acceptance of our experience wherever possible. A positive sign of spiritual progression is that we practise more absolute acceptance, which leads to less of a need to practise relative acceptance. Absolute acceptance allows us to be at peace with what has been, what is now and what is to come.

Options for Cultivating Acceptance

There are two options we can take for cultivating acceptance. The first is that we follow paths and general guidance laid out in spiritual teachings on how to live an ethical life. Over time, this will help us to set up the conditions in our life to let go of resistance and we will naturally become more accepting as a result. This book contains pointers that can help with this.

Examples include caring for the body, connecting with nature, establishing a meditation practice, spiritual friendship, simplicity and releasing addictions. The second option is to work on our connection with Presence here and now in this moment.

It can be interesting to consider these options for cultivating acceptance, but in the end it does not really matter which angle you come from. Personally, without any conscious planning, I have cultivated greater levels of acceptance using both options. Firstly, I have made direct changes to my life and worked on training my mind to become more accepting, using guidance from spiritual teachings. Secondly, I have also worked on becoming more Present now using some of the guidance contained in this book and through the teachings of Eckhart Tolle [1]. Your personal route to acceptance has already been decided for you. It may be that, as you understand these two options, it starts to become clear as to where you need to place more effort in the future.

A dogmatic belief is that the only way to become awakened or fully Present is to follow a certain path as laid out in a set of spiritual teachings or religion. Some people are *driven* to reach their goal, placing all their efforts into a given path. A person who is driven has obsessive or compulsive characteristics in relation to their spiritual goal, which hinders progress as it creates excessive thinking. Having *drive* on the other hand helps. With drive, the discipline and self-motivation is there to progress without the attachment to the end result. The practitioners that are driven and lost in thought, who are not true practitioners, actually miss out on the opportunity to live, be Present and enjoy who they really are. Their relationship to the path will become a hindrance in its own right, causing harm to themselves and others. This can apply to groups as well as individuals. Those that have drive and are motivated towards their goal without becoming identified with it make far more progress. We all have "Presence", "God" and "Buddha Nature" within us now. The blocker is the vale of thought that surrounds it.

We do not need to think at all to be Present as Presence transcends thought. I remember when I was ardently training to become an ordained Buddhist. Occasionally people would say to me, "You don't need to do all that meditation or all those retreats and study. They are unnecessary. You can be Present right now." I used to react to these comments with feelings of annoyance for two reasons. The first was because these people did not understand the path that I was taking and were as such not really qualified to comment on it. The second, and this is what used to bite the most, was despite them not understanding, there was some truth in what they said!

One extreme is to be obsessively lost within a spiritual path or religion. Another extreme is to fail to take any responsibility for a dysfunctional life and spiritual progress. I remember trying to be Present before following a spiritual path. It was not even possible for me to understand how to be Present. I was not ready and was continuously lost in thought. I connected with a religious movement for a few years and sought help from therapists, which helped make positive changes to my life and ways of thinking. I then let go of my involvement with the religious movement and continued my spiritual journey independently. This was my path and I appreciate that yours may be different.

Some people are in a stronger position where they need very little in terms of a path to follow and can practise being Present straight away. Others, myself included, benefit from opting for the structure of a religious organization for a period of time, whilst others choose to devote their entire life to a given path or religion. I cannot advise you on the route you should take, but hopefully, through reading this book, that route should become clearer. The secret here is to establish a balance. We need to balance taking responsibility for our thoughts and conditions whilst knowing and developing our ability to become Present more and more of the time.

Acceptance of Our Relative Self

There are two types of self. The first is our absolute self or true self, which is formless Presence. The second is our relative self, which is our form-based self as a person, including our body, name, roles, thoughts and personal history. The ego does not understand the absolute self and will never accept the relative self. If the ego were to understand the absolute self, it would realize it is no longer required and cease to exist. The ego keeps itself alive through its ignorance of the true self and dissatisfaction of the relative self through craving for things to be fixed or different to how they are now. The ego will always want us to gain something, lose something or grasp onto something.

I am not a naturally sociable person in groups by any stretch of the imagination. My preference is to be in solitude or with people on a one-to-one basis. I have no preference to socialize in groups and will only be motivated to do so if I am called upon for altruistic reasons or to serve others. If I am with a group of people having dinner, my default mode will be to sit there quietly and observe what is going on. I will interact if somebody speaks to me or if I need to say something, with the intention of helping somebody or the group as a whole. Occasionally, I will be more talkative and sociable if I am taking a particular role such as attending a business meal or taking responsibility for training a group of people. I can do this by consciously playing the role, but it is outside of my natural preferences aligned with my character. I have learned over time that if I am required to socialize and can surrender fully, I will be at peace and even enjoy this type of interaction with others.

For many years, my ego wanted me to be somebody I was not. It would compare my relative self to others that were naturally more extroverted and charismatic. These were the types of people who can socialize effortlessly with groups and a wide range of people in different contexts. My ego's opinion was that these social geniuses were getting more attention and love. Through its own greed, my ego was creating feelings of envy. Wherever you find envy, you find one or more underlying attachments. In this case, I was attached to the belief that I should be popular and liked in whatever group I frequented in order to feel good about myself. I was envious of those who I perceived were getting what I believed should be mine. For a long time, I also believed that to be successful and worthy, I should be 'better' than others, and tried to prove this through creating mental stories that compared myself favourably to them. When I met people who were in and around my social groups and who were more talented in certain areas that my ego deemed to be important, I would react by feeling inferior. The ego loved this as it was creating a sense of separateness with the people I was comparing myself to. It was also creating beliefs about my 'self' that it could identify with. The suffering my ego was creating was as a direct consequence of not accepting my relative self.

Once I had brought acceptance to this part of my relative self, I was free from any associated comparisons, judgements and suffering. I was then able to allow my energy to flow more freely into activities that suited my strengths and talents.

At the same time, I was open to my relative self changing. I finally reached this point of self-acceptance by accessing and reflecting upon spiritual teachings, which helped me understand how the ego operates. Hearing inspiring people talk about their own shortcomings so openly helped me to realize that we are all unique and wired differently, based upon our genetics and past conditioning. We all have our own talents and areas where we are deficient relative to others. We are not really deficient. The absolute self is always absolutely fine and we are as we are. The ego believes we are deficient based upon its judgements.

If we can get our head around the difference between the absolute self and relative self, acceptance of who we are demonstrates an understanding that our faults are not associated with us, i.e., the absolute self. Our faults are simply ego-based judgements associated with the relative self, which is an evolutionary work in progress. This understanding creates a space between the two selves and directly enables Presence. When we take responsibility for our actions, this is the absolute self taking responsibility for the relative self. It represents all that the spiritual life consists of. Ultimately, once full responsibility has been taken, the two selves merge into one, the duality is released and we become wholly Present.

By understanding this deeply enough and accepting our relative self in this way it is much easier to accept the relative self of others and helps us to acknowledge their positive qualities. We accept their relative self from the absolute self. There is only one absolute self, which is present in everybody. The one absolute self accepts the many relative selves. If we can see others and ourself clearly as being connected and working together to evolve, comparisons and related judgements fall away naturally. Through accepting perceived shortcomings rather than resisting them we become Present. With my own shortcomings, of which I have many, I am always impressed how easy it is to feel at peace after I have accepted them and reconnected with who I truly am. As a side benefit, acceptance of shortcomings puts us in the best possible position to transcend them if that is what is required of us.

The Four A's Cycle

Through Presence, we experience a natural cycle of awareness, acceptance and appropriate action. Something enters our awareness. It might be bodily sensations, sense perceptions, feelings or thoughts. The first step is to be aware of that experience. Through awareness of our experience, we start to understand some of the basic facts about existence, which helps us to accept things. We learn that things are impermanent and constantly in a state of flux. We learn that because of this, nothing is ultimately satisfying. We learn that everything is connected and can be changed through contact. We learn that if we get lost in thought and identify with things, we suffer. We can read about all of this in spiritual books and listen to talks on the Internet or a retreat, which can be helpful, but the most effective way to understand is through our own experience. Our own experience contains a colossal amount of examples and demonstrations for us to learn from. Understanding the truths about our existence on an intellectual level is helpful, but not enough. By staying aware and experiencing examples of how things really are, we can understand at a level of depth that allows us to bring acceptance to anything. An intellectual understanding evolves into a knowing.

Once we are aware of our experience or situation, we then take the second step, which is to accept it. If we are aware, we are Present and if we are Present, we can accept anything within our experience. That includes unpleasant feelings. It is the ego that resists things when we are lost in thought. When we are not thinking or when our thinking manifests through Presence, everything is accepted because resistance can only survive when it is fuelled by ungoverned thought. Once we cut off its fuel supply, it passes immediately.

We must fully accept our experience or situation in whatever shape or form it takes. Once we are accepting, we can then take the third step, which is to choose what appropriate action we take as a result. This completes the Four A's Cycle: Awareness, acceptance and appropriate action. The action can be thinking, speech, physical action or a combination of all three. It might also be to do nothing at all. When we follow the Four A's Cycle, the decision on appropriate action is taken wisely and consciously. If we examine our own experience we will see this route being followed during times when we are Present. The action is fully aligned with what the universe required from us at the time to help us evolve and contribute towards the wider evolution of consciousness in others. It cultivates peace and love. On the contrary, when we are lost in thought, we lack awareness and are in a state of resistance. In these cases, the cycle of Presence is broken and taken over by the ego causing us to become unskilful through habitual and reactive action, which ultimately causes harm.

You might be able to recall times when you have taken action in the past without accepting a situation, which has been problematic to yourself or others. If a work colleague has said something that offended you in some way, you might feel angry. If you deny the feeling of anger or believe that your colleague should have done something different to what they did, any action you take will be fuelled with negativity and resistance. By accepting fully that the colleague said what they said and that you were angry positions you to respond wisely and compassionately. You might tell the colleague how you felt after they said what they did, but take responsibility for your own feelings rather than judging their action as bad.

The Four A's Cycle starts with awareness. Everything begins there. Awareness is essential. It is impossible to accept something that we are not aware of or cannot see clearly. We can only accept something once we know what we are accepting. Once we have cultivated awareness, acceptance is much easier to practise and through acceptance flows appropriate action.

POINTS FOR REFLECTION

- Thoughts do not need to be judged, controlled or pushed away and should never be viewed as bad or wrong.

- When we fully accept things as they are, including thoughts, feelings, bodily sensations and external situations, we are free from suffering.

- Through acceptance, our level of fear reduces and we can enjoy a real sense of confidence, lightness and freedom.

- The intention must always be to accept what is happening in the present moment and take action when required to positively influence the future.

- Through acceptance, we can become peaceful, aligned with the present moment and in touch with who we really are.

- Acceptance aligns us with exactly how things are now, which puts us in the best possible place to respond appropriately to whatever is required.

- It is the ego that resists things and never our true essence. Our true essence is always accepting, as all things need to be accepted.

- Resisting something means that we are craving for the universe to be different to how it already is.

- The body reacts to resistance with tension and illness, so through being more accepting we significantly increase our chances of staying physically well.

- Many people believe that control as a reaction to resistance provides power. They are wrong. Acceptance and the present moment provide power.

- At the point of acceptance, we are fully aligned with everything that has happened in our experience beforehand and everything that may happen in the future.

- Acceptance and Presence go together. Put another way, acceptance is Presence.

- Resistance pushes us out of the present moment into the realm of time and creates stress.

- If we become aware of certain situations leading us to a state of resistance, then we should investigate the causes and either bring acceptance to them or change our conditions.

- There are two types of self. The first is our absolute self or true self, which is formless Presence. The second is our relative self, which is us in our form as a person, including our body, name, roles, thoughts and personal history.

- The absolute self is always absolutely fine.

- The ego does not understand the absolute self and will never accept the relative self.

- Relative acceptance is conceptual and based in the realm of time.

- Absolute acceptance is a real-time, here-and-now practice in the present moment requiring no conceptualization or consideration of time.

- The more we can practise absolute acceptance, the less we need to practise relative acceptance.

- A positive sign of spiritual progression is that we practise more absolute acceptance, which leads to less of a need to practise relative acceptance.

- The only real acceptance is acceptance of the present moment, which is absolute acceptance.

- Part of our practice is to be the love around absolutely everything including what we dislike or find unpleasant.

- Acceptance only really applies to the present moment. The past has gone and the future does not exist yet.

- Our vision should be to consistently accept our experience and respond to ourself with love.

- We can remind ourself that we are human beings with our own past conditioning and know that we are works in progress just like everybody else. If we reflect on this truth, we will soon become more accepting of ourself.

- We do not need to think at all to be Present as Presence transcends thought.

- Through Presence, we experience a natural cycle of awareness, acceptance and appropriate action.

OPTIONAL LEARNING ACTIVITIES

- Investigate and make a list of your regular themes of resistance. For each theme, ask yourself under what situations or with whom do you find yourself in a state of resistance? Is it possible to bring acceptance to these situations or do changes need to be made?

- When you are meditating or spending time in stillness, bring awareness to what you are resisting. This may be a thought, feeling, bodily sensation or something entering the senses. When this happens, make a mental label along the lines of "I am resisting this thought" or "I am resisting this feeling". Then accept the experience and allow it to pass naturally. This is practising absolute acceptance.

- Next time you find yourself in a challenging situation, take a moment to stop and bring the Four A's Cycle to mind: Awareness, acceptance & appropriate action. Ask yourself the questions:
    - "Am I aware of my experience?"
    - "Am I accepting of my experience?"
    - Once you are confident that you are aware and accepting of your experience ask yourself:
    - "What is the appropriate action (which may be no action) to take now?"

Chapter Ten

Work & Service

Presence can be integrated into our work and any activity where we are serving others. This may be a paid job, voluntary work, cooking a meal for our family or listening to a friend. We are often presented with spontaneous opportunities to serve through connection with others. Examples might include slowing down our driving to allow somebody to exit from a busy junction, listening to a person who is sitting next to us on the bus who needs to talk or giving money to a beggar on the street.

When we are Present more of the time, we are allowing the Presence to flow through us and guide us. We can metaphorically take our grasping hands off the steering wheel and allow the power from the present moment to do the steering. The direction is often away from craving form-based pleasure and towards service. The pleasure may still be enjoyed when it is presented to us and at the same time, we are free from our dependence upon it. A life that revolves around service means taking responsibility for ourself, as we need to be in a good state in order to serve others effectively. In fact, serving ourself and serving others are the same in absolute terms. Note that service may not mean doing anything in particular. It can be as simple as being Present amongst others without doing anything at all which in itself is a valued contribution. It goes without saying that the most important factor in our work and service is Presence. Being Present when we are undertaking our activities is primary. The type of activities we are involved in and what manifests from them are secondary. Any activity that we undertake will be skilful if it comes from a state of Presence. Activity and Presence need each other. Activity requires Presence so that it can be aligned with what is required to help raise consciousness as a whole. Presence requires activity so that it can manifest itself through form.

Conflicting & Complementary Views

I have observed in my own career that one of the tickets to success is to build the capacity to hold views that appear to conflict when in fact they are complementary. I remember presenting a business strategy to a group of directors. After the presentation, the strategy was deemed critical to the future success of the business. I prepared diligently for that presentation and delivered it well. At the same time I did not really mind if the strategy made any real difference. Similarly, I honoured and respected that particular consultancy contract whilst knowing I would have been just fine if I had to let go of it.

We have to learn to honour and respect all aspects of our work whilst maintaining perspective. The perspective is at the level of the cosmos allowing us to see that in the grand scheme of things it is usually not going to make a significant difference whether we achieve this or that. When we observe the vastness of the universe and contemplate the infinite nature of time, we see our own little life as a speck of dust. It may not feel like that most of the time when we are lost in our own thoughts about personal dramas and everything revolving around us. It may help to ask ourself "Will this matter in one year, ten years or one hundred years from now?" Ironically, when we can hold these conflicting and complementary views by honouring things whilst seeing the insignificance of them we find that we become happier and more effective at work and everything else we get involved in. If we hold the two views simultaneously, we can perform our activities with quality, peace and lightness.

The Three Modalities of Awakened Doing

In *The New Earth*[4], Eckhart Tolle introduces 'the three modalities of awakened doing'. Over the next few pages I would like to share my personal interpretation, experiences and application of his teaching. We are always in one of four modalities when undertaking any activity: resistance, acceptance, enjoyment or enthusiasm. How we choose to conduct our day-to-day activities, including work and service, influences whether we are Present (accepting, enjoying or enthusiastic) or lost in thought (resisting).

If we are lost in thought whilst doing an activity, we are resisting it. When we are in a state of resistance, we may detest or deny the activity. Other characteristics of resistance include suffering, unskilfulness and unhappiness. Resistance enables a flow of negative, contaminated energy into whatever we do and create. What we do create from a state of resistance is not true creation as true creation can only come through Presence. In resistance, we merely produce rather than create and the quality of what we produce during those times is low. The amount of stress we experience is proportionate to the amount of resistance we have to the present moment.

The antidotes to resistance are either to fully accept the activity or to let go of it. We must avoid being stuck in the middle and looping around an activity we are resisting again and again, as indicated by the 'Continue' loop in my illustration below. Some people do this for years and even lifetimes. They continue with the same activities or situations that are causing them to suffer. The only chance they get to change is when the suffering created by the resistance is so high that it wakes them up to take action. Fortunately, we do not have to wait that long and we have a choice now.

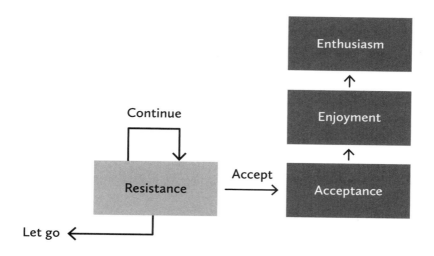

Darren's graphical interpretation of Tolle's Modalities of Awakened Doing

Resistance can enter the world of work and service in many guises and some reflection or analysis may be required to determine its root cause. It can be easy to misinterpret a situation so we need to understand what is really going on. On a number of occasions, I recall working in a modality of resistance, being regularly lost in thought and experiencing an internal dialogue about how I must leave my job or stop working altogether. This internal dialogue happened in parallel with completing my duties. Frustratingly, the quality of my work and relationships would suffer and then cause further problems, leading to yet more suffering and resistance. Once I was able to bring acceptance to the situation or move away from it, I could continue to work peacefully.

Despite most of my jobs being intellectual rather than involving physical labour, one of my biggest challenges with work has been managing the body. When I find myself in resistance at work, it is often because I am tired or physically unwell. Once I regain Presence, I stop what I am doing and turn my attention to the body. Just a few seconds of stillness and body awareness is all that is required. Usually, I find there is something requiring attention. It may be an ache, pain, uncomfortable sitting posture, hunger or tiredness manifesting as heavy eyes or a foggy head. Because I was lost in thought, I had lost connectivity and awareness with the body. Once I understood that the body needed attention, I would sometimes take action to support it by resting, sleeping, eating or taking medication. On some occasions, it was impractical to do this if I was working with others or had deadlines to meet. Often, I consciously decided to work whilst experiencing the physical symptoms and in those cases I made a determined effort to accept the situation fully. I would say to myself "I accept that I am tired and I will continue working" and a transformation would occur within me that shifted the modality from resistance to acceptance. Awareness of our experience will often lead to acceptance. We know when we are in the modality of acceptance as resisting thoughts cease or thoughts cease altogether. If our mind is quiet, it is impossible to resist the situation as resistance manifests through thought.

Some causes of resistance at work are light and quick to pass whilst others are deeper and sustained. In the example above, the tiredness was usually short-term and caused by inappropriate food or insufficient sleep or rest. When the causes are deeper and sustained, they require further investigation. For example, if we are regularly tired or ill whilst working, this could be due to an underlying medical condition, a lifestyle issue or emotional issues.

The next modality is acceptance, which signifies Presence. When we accept and surrender to our activities, we complete them peacefully regardless of whether we find them pleasant or unpleasant. There are no thoughts about why we should not be doing something or what else we could be doing. Instead, there is peace and concentration, which allows the activity to be completed in alignment with the present moment, willingly, and with quality. Often, we can transform our state of resistance into acceptance whilst completing activities. This can happen instantly or it might take time to cultivate. If we do not bring acceptance to an activity straight away, we may want to give ourself a chance to try it a few more times before letting it go. It is often worth placing a time-scale against a quest for acceptance to ensure that we do not get stuck in the resistance loop for longer than is necessary.

I recall being in resistance whenever I needed to mow the lawn in my garden. This happened for years and it caused a great deal of suffering. I recall feelings of anxiety and my mind worrying excessively about all sorts of things whilst I was pushing the lawn mower back and forth. The reality of the situation was that everything was fine. I was out in the fresh air, around nature and moving my body, which are all nourishing. Once I understood more about acceptance, I made a conscious effort to surrender to the activity and let go of the thoughts that were creating the suffering. After working on this for a while, the acceptance gradually pervaded the experience. After that, I would even have the occasional moment of enjoyment whilst mowing the lawn. I went through exactly the same process with washing the dishes! Introducing basic techniques such as keeping some awareness anchored to the breath or body helps. Also, changing how, when or where we do the activity may help us to cultivate acceptance.

If we try diligently and cannot bring acceptance to an activity, then we must consider letting it go and freeing ourself and others from the suffering created through our involvement. This can be difficult, especially when letting go is incompatible with the desires of others. People may complain or judge us, which can trigger feelings of irrational guilt. I let go of a number of relationships that caused sustained suffering which felt unresolvable at the time. I would often let go suddenly or harshly, which harmed those I was moving away from. Over the years, I have practised being more considerate and gentler if I need to distance or remove myself from others due to my sustained resistance. When I look back, I can see that the suddenness in moving away was due to resisting and suffering for too long, causing me to get to a point where I would erupt emotionally. The learning here is to be aware of our resistance as early as possible, placing us in a better position to resolve it with kindness.

I recall drinking alcohol on a daily basis. Personally, there was no way I could bring acceptance to that. It was impossible for me to consume alcohol and stay Present. The mind would wander and become lost in thought. Emotions would be triggered unmanageably. This would sometimes stay confined to my inner experience and more often than not it would leak out through contaminated communication. Sometimes the suffering caused would be subtle and at other times it would be significant. In the end, after much suffering, I let go. If I knew about these spiritual teachings at the time I am confident I would have let go of that addiction much quicker and suffered less as a result.

We must be kind to ourself and never view a conscious exit from an activity, situation or relationship as a failure. It is perfectly natural in life to move away from some things and towards others. We should always take time after letting go of an activity, relationship or removing ourself from a situation to reflect on the reasons for our resistance. This enables learning and frees us up from getting ourself into a similar situation again. Once we are in tune with the way things need to be, we can use our awareness of resistance and acceptance to guide us on our path towards a peaceful and happier life. If we are living in acceptance, we are aligned with our true purpose regardless of the content of our life and changes in circumstances.

If we have a requirement to work, we may ask ourself whether we are in the right job. How do we know if we are in the right job? It is impossible to make any conclusions because our minds are incapable of processing all the causes and effects relating to the work we do and how that ripples out into the rest of the universe. We can only be aware and process a tiny fragment of the continuous stream of conditions. That said, we can determine whether we are in the wrong job. A wrong job is a job that causes us to be in an excessive amount of resistance, which cannot be transformed into acceptance. Resistance causes harm. If we are bringing harm to ourself or others in the work that we do, then we are in the wrong job. The practice is to be aware of whether we are in a modality of resistance or acceptance in our work and strive to be in a state of acceptance for as much of the time as possible.

Some activities we accept can also be enjoyed, which adds an increased aliveness and joyfulness. Many things we are already doing can be enjoyed. A simple example where I experienced changes in modality was washing the dishes. For many years, I experienced resistance. Through practising staying Present and being aware of my direct experience at the time, I was able to accept washing the dishes and then progressed to enjoying it. It never fails to surprise me when a simple activity that I may originally view as dull or boring transforms into something that I can enjoy. I experienced the same phenomenon with ironing shirts. We can turn these simple activities into enjoyable meditations. We should not expect to enjoy every activity. Some activities may be completed with acceptance only and that is fine. We can allow the enjoyment to arise naturally.

Finally, we come to enthusiasm, which is present during activities that involve a more intense aliveness. Activities that we are enthusiastic about are creative, containing a goal we are working towards and the direct or indirect involvement of others. When we are experiencing enthusiasm, the journey towards the goal is intensely enjoyable. There may be a plan for the goal to be completed by a particular date or time, but the ego does not crave for it to be completed. When we hit obstacles on our way to achieving the goal, we work around them and transform any negative energy that blocks the goal into positive energy that helps us to move forward. Enthusiasm comes and goes through the conditions and energies we have at different times of our life.

For me, writing and working towards promoting this book has been an enthusiastic experience. It has been creative, working towards a goal and involved many others along the way. I hope that it will connect with more people over the coming years. There has been negligible resistance involved in the process, mainly a positive flow of energy and intense aliveness during the activity. I have encountered blockers along the way. People who I would like to help me not helping me. Deadlines that I was hoping for not being met. There has always been an acceptance and flow of energy around these issues. It has felt like a higher power has been directing the resolution of these issues and I am playing my part in resolving them through accepting whatever arises.

Another source of enthusiasm for me is serving my children. If they need anything I immediately find the energy to help them. It could be helping them prepare a CV, giving them food or providing a lift in my car. Anything really. When they ask for something, I like to get onto it as soon as I can. It feels very natural and enjoyable to help them. I notice other parents doing the same. There is a creative element to parenting in that through serving your children in the right way you are working with them to influence and create their future.

Enthusiasm and enjoyment should not be forced. All that is needed to be Present, which is our real objective, is awareness and acceptance. It helps to cultivate a lightness and openness as to whether we experience enjoyment and enthusiasm. If we gaze at a rainbow when the conditions are just right, we will observe when the light of the sun disperses in the rain. If it is appropriate at the time, enjoyment will flow naturally without being forced. Or we may just accept what we see peacefully and that is how it is.

Concentration

Concentration is essential to enable quality to flow into our activities and is independent of Presence. To illustrate the independence, we can use two example scenarios. The first is somebody who is concentrating on carrying out a violent act towards another person. Their concentration and single-pointedness may be there, but they will not be Present. Presence is always vacant in a person's actions when harm is being caused. The second example is of somebody concentrating on an activity to help another person without the expectation of anything in return. In this second example, there is concentration, love and therefore Presence.

Concentration can be used as a gateway into Presence. A tactic to enable us to regain Presence when we are lost in thought is to concentrate on a single object. The object could be something external to us such as a flower, or something within us such as a thought or feeling. It could also be concentration on a single activity or process such as walking, writing or polishing our shoes. A natural consequence of concentration is that we are no longer lost in thought as the process of concentration aligns and organizes thoughts around the object or activity and from there we can be Present. High-quality work requires concentration so it follows that producing high-quality work is an indirect gateway into Presence.

Identifications at Work

To be Present, it does not matter what work activity we do so long as it is skilful and we are not identified with it. Many people are identified with a number of different aspects of their work. The identifications may be positively or negatively related to wealth, fame, responsibility, relationships, attention or appreciation. All of these things are absolutely fine in their own right but become harmful when we identify with them and believe they are who we are. They cannot be who we are in our true essence as these things are changeable, whereas who we truly are does not change.

So how are these identifications created? They are attachments formed as an escape from pain. For example, if we do not feel good about ourself at a point in time, rather than dealing with the root cause and experiencing the pain to release it, we may identify with something successful we experience at work and use it to prop up our self-esteem. I recall delivering a presentation at a conference and sharing my plans to transform a particular area within the organization I was working. The Managing Director was so impressed that he asked me to present the same plan at a number of other conferences scheduled over the coming months. So I went on to present my plan to lots of people and received their support. My ego loved this and whilst doing so, I unknowingly identified with being the creative guy with the great idea. This identification was created because I felt a lack of confidence and was anxious at conferences. The positive view I had of myself was not who I really was, but an opinion I had created and attached to so that I could feel confident and important. Unfortunately for my ego, a short while after, when the plan was presented to the board, they decided against starting the project at that point in time. I quickly changed from feeling like a hero to feeling like a loser! I experienced a lot of anxiety around that decision and even considered whether I should find another job and was blaming others for the situation. It makes me chuckle now when I look back because it was such a great learning experience.

There are numerous other forms of identification that can be created at work and when we are faced with the opportunity, we will always take one of two paths. If we are fortunate enough to be Present, we will take the wise path. The wise path is to experience the underlying pain the ego is using as a trigger to create the identification and use that moment as an opportunity to heal. The unwise path is to escape from the pain by creating the identification.

Reviewing Work & Service

If we refer to religions and spiritual teachers, we may hear all sorts of different opinions about the amount of work we should undertake and the type of work we should be engaged in. Arguments can be put forward for doing an inordinate amount of work, doing no work or something in-between. What we need to make spiritual progress to date has already been given to us and what we need going forward will also be given to us. People get lost in thought complaining about their work situation. Such thoughts and discussion come from a place of craving for change and refusal to accept what is, which reinforces the ego.

It is fine to change our work situation as long as we do so peacefully and from a place of acceptance. This means the energy that flows into the new work situation will be positive. During my career I have interviewed many people. After asking a number of questions, I soon get a sense for whether they have brought acceptance to the situation at their last place of work. I deduce this from the answers they provide and the energy I feel within their communication. If we can bring acceptance to a job before we move to the next, it makes the future lighter and happier. The same is true of relationships, assets or any other situation that we wish to change. Where practical, we should always bring acceptance to the current situation before changing it. That said, as discussed earlier, there are times when we do need to remove ourselves from a situation if acceptance is not possible for us at the time.

There are some pointers we can take into consideration regarding our work. We have basic needs, which must be taken into account. Asking ourself the following questions about our work situation may help us to determine whether things need to change:

- Does my current work schedule allow me to have enough time to rest and sleep?
- Have I got enough time outside of work to undertake activities that I deem to be essential? These might include exercise, meditation, creative activities, spending time with friends and family, pursuing spiritual goals and other forms of service.
- Does my work situation make it difficult for me to stay Present and skilful?
- Are the earnings from work meeting my needs and the needs of those who are financially dependent upon me?
- Am I making sufficient provision for my long-term financial requirements, taking responsibility for how I will fund myself and fund those financially dependent upon me when I am retired?
- Is my work leading to the creation of products or services that are going to cause others harm, for example, manufacturing cigarettes or helping provide a service that encourages people to gamble?
- Does the work I am undertaking support the maintenance of a healthy body?

In summary, taking responsibility for our work situation is part of our spiritual practice. This requires ongoing monitoring as our work situation and personal needs are always subject to change.

POINTS FOR REFLECTION

- A life that revolves around service means taking responsibility for ourself, as we need to be in a good state in order to serve others effectively.

- Presence requires activity so that it can manifest itself through form.

- The ideal we should be working towards is to fully integrate Presence into every activity.

- We have to learn to honour and respect all aspects of our work whilst maintaining perspective.

- We are in one of four modalities when undertaking any activity: resistance, acceptance, enjoyment or enthusiasm.

- If we are lost in thought whilst undertaking an activity, we are resisting it.

- Resistance enables a flow of negative, contaminated energy into what we do and create.

- The antidotes to resistance are either to accept the activity or to stop doing it.

- The amount of stress we experience is proportionate to the amount of resistance we have to the present moment.

- We know when we are in the modality of acceptance as resisting thoughts cease or thoughts cease altogether.

- We should not expect to enjoy every activity. Some activities may be completed with acceptance only and that is fine.

- Enthusiasm is present during activities that involve an even more intense aliveness than with enjoyment. Activities that we are enthusiastic about are creative, containing a goal we are working towards and the direct or indirect involvement of others.

- If we try diligently and cannot bring acceptance to an activity, then we must consider letting it go and freeing ourself and others from the suffering created through our involvement.

- We should be aware of our resistance as early as possible, placing us in a better position to let go of it skilfully.

- If we are living in acceptance, we are aligned with our true purpose regardless of the content of our life.

- A tactic to enable us to regain Presence when we are lost in thought is to concentrate on a single object or activity.

- High-quality work requires concentration and concentration is a gateway into Presence.

- To be Present, it does not matter what activity we do as long as it is skilful and we are not identified with it.

- A wrong job is a job that causes us to be in an excessive amount of resistance, which cannot be transformed into acceptance.

- If we are bringing harm to ourself or others in the work we do, then we are in the wrong job.

- All that is needed to be Present, which is our real objective, is awareness and acceptance.

OPTIONAL LEARNING ACTIVITIES

- Make a list of your various activities categorising them into the modalities: resistance, acceptance, enjoyment and enthusiasm.

- For activities where you are in resistance, consider how you can bring acceptance to them taking into account how, when, where or with whom you do the activities.

- Consider peacefully letting go of activities that you cannot bring acceptance to. For significant activities, ensure that you have taken the time to explore if acceptance is possible before considering how you can let go of them skilfully.

- Review your work situation using the questions listed earlier in the chapter.

Chapter Eleven

Teachers, Religion & Study

Spiritual teachings from the written or spoken word will at best provide us with pointers to the truth. Language is not rich enough to fully explain a subject such as Presence, God or Enlightenment. Even with this constraint, teachings are useful and can open our minds to an intelligence that goes beyond thought. We can receive spiritual teachings through other gateways including nature. The stillness of a tree, the impermanence of an ocean or the insubstantiality of the breath all point to the truth and teach us how things really are.

Until we are fully awakened, anything in the world of form can teach us to become more Present. As individuals, groups, nations or the collective whole we may occasionally appear to be going backward from a spiritual standpoint, but over time, it will always be evident that the perceived backward step will, in fact, enable us to move forward. This ranges from small mistakes we make on an individual level to the mass unconsciousness demonstrated through war. Suffering at any level is a great teacher. The progression arising from suffering helps us to accept and be grateful for our whole experience. Learning through suffering must never be used as justification or an excuse for acting unskilfully. We must never create suffering for others or ourself intentionally. If suffering manifests naturally, we can learn from it and be grateful for the experience.

Spiritual Teachers & Religious Movements

We may connect with a spiritual teacher through a book, the Internet or in person. For a period of time they can appear to represent a perfect match for our needs. We may also create an attachment and view the teacher as someone who is going to meet our spiritual needs for the rest of our lives. This process is analogous to that of a romance early on in a personal relationship. Some people choose to commit their life to serving a teacher and become their disciples. Many religions advise people to stick to one teacher and one set of teachings on the basis that digging a single well deeply for the rest of our life will take us spiritually further than digging many shallow wells. No single teacher will ultimately satisfy our entire spiritual needs. Our needs and the teacher will change over time. Also, spiritual needs are met through a variety of different forms in addition to teachers.

There are teachings within and around everything we gravitate towards and everything that gravitates towards us, including people, situations, and experiences that we may initially misjudge as bad. Over time, if we are aware, we may see how these conditions have helped us to progress. With this in mind, we should honour our teachers and show gratitude to them along with everything and everybody else that we encounter, as all this is enabling us to move forward. This principle can be applied to our enemies. The experience we have with enemies also guides us, which makes them spiritual teachers too.

If a spiritual teacher advises us specifically to do this or that, they are indirectly claiming they know what is 'best' for us. They do not fully understand our past and the infinite ways in which the future can unfold for us, so how do they know which path we should take? There is no 'best' action or any real choice. There is simply a process, which takes everybody and everything into consideration. A teacher, religion or movement cannot possibly comprehend this whole process fully unless they have transcended to a level that we would not even be able to validate. Any unenlightened being, which is most people on the planet, that claims they know what is best for us either directly or indirectly is demonstrating their ignorance. A person can never represent a perfect teacher and a set of scriptures can never represent the complete teachings. The cosmos ensures that we receive the teachings we need when we need them. The source of all spiritual teachings is infinite. As you are reading now, your teachings are the words in this paragraph.

The whole process of spiritual development is very mysterious. It may feel as though teachers and teachings find us without us even looking for them as we attune to what we need at the time. Associating with one teacher may link us to another or take us on a completely different path. What is truly magical about this process is that we are all going through it. The whole universe is arranged and continues to be arranged to accommodate everybody's spiritual progression, regardless of whether they are consciously making an effort to become more Present. It can be a difficult pill to swallow for some, but all the horrid things that happen, the pain and suffering that is experienced, is part of this process. Over time and as we all become more conscious, the overall suffering experienced by humanity will reduce, as it has done over the centuries. Ultimately the suffering will be removed altogether and in the meantime, it is a necessary cost of progress.

There is no magic formula for selecting a religion or teacher and it may be that for periods of time we consciously decide to be free of them. Religions and teachers will always be limited as it is impossible for them to provide us with the whole truth. This is because the truth cannot be communicated. It can only be known. Teachers and religions provide pointers to the truth through various means such as exemplification, words, and rituals. Our job as spiritual practitioners is to be receptive to and follow these pointers when they are relevant. They are all pointing to the same place. Some people report profound experiences through specific teachings or their own suffering that enable them to become awakened instantly. For the majority of us, we awaken gradually through practice. When we follow the pointers that are accessible through religion, teachers and our own experience (including suffering), we make a connection with the truth. We are then likely to lose that connection shortly afterwards and regain it again at some point in the future, which is all part of the process. Over time, our goal is to increase the amount of time we reside in the truth or Presence, with the ultimate ideal of being Present continuously. This is what the Buddhists call enlightenment or awakening.

Religious movements often provide people with helpful structures and support. Some of the most religiously devoted people are those whose lives were in great trouble and filled with suffering before they became religious. People join religious movements for all sorts of reasons. Poverty can motivate somebody to join if the movement offers food and shelter. Internal conditions, including mental health issues and addictions, also motivate people to reach out to movements for support. Others get involved because the movement provides true friendship, which they may not have experienced previously. I have met people in religious movements who believed that without joining them, they would have ended up insane or dead through drug abuse, some other addiction or mental illness. For these people, the structure and support is ideal. As a result, their levels of gratitude and devotion are often so high that they go on to make great progress. Others, whose lives are more stable, may connect with religious movements mainly due to their natural resonance with the teachings, teachers and values.

Given that everything is here to help us become more Present, what is the point of making any effort to connect with spiritual teachers and study their teachings? Every decision that we make in life, no matter how small, represents a T-junction which influences the amount of suffering we will experience in the future. Taking on board some of the pointers from this book and other teachings will help us to become more skilful and Present, which means we suffer less. Each turn at the T-junctions may challenge us. If we take the unskilful route, sooner or later, through our suffering, we will learn and make a wiser decision next time. If we take the skilful route, we will suffer less and be happier. The truth is that we are empowered to make that choice on every occasion.

We may experience doubt during the process of selecting a spiritual teacher or within an existing student-teacher relationship. This can be doubt in the teacher's style, their religion, the teachings themselves or doubt in our own ability to work with them. This is absolutely normal and the response should be to investigate the causes. Asking questions of ourself, our teacher and wise friends helps us to understand what is triggering our feelings and what action we may need to take. We can create space and time when it comes to dealing with doubt. There should be no time pressure in deciding if we need to continue or let go of an existing student-teacher relationship. The same goes for a relationship with a religious movement. Be careful not to make any rash decisions driven by emotions or temporary conditions. A rounded decision will take into account the facts of the situation, the experience we can draw upon and our intuition. Once these are aligned, which may take a little time, we will be confident with our decision. This process may be applied to any decision.

We must never expect to be ultimately satisfied by a religion or teacher for two reasons. The first reason is that like us, the religion and teacher are all subject to change. What we may be delighted with at one time may change and disappoint us at another. The second reason is that all unenlightened humans are involved in the awakening process meaning that teachers may be unskilful at times. They are not perfect. Within any religion, we can guarantee that the vast majority, if not all the authoritative figures within the hierarchy will not be awakened. They will become lost in thought and act unskilfully just like everybody else. For those who are more evolved, this will be less frequent, but always a possibility. This should not necessarily stop us from joining a religious movement. Whatever decision we take, there will be benefits and risks involved. We should investigate the facts, ask questions and then make an informed decision. That way, if we do get involved in a religious movement or work with a specific teacher, we do so with our eyes open.

I remember deciding to let go of working towards joining a religious movement that I was involved with for many years. It took me over a year from the point of where I first experienced serious feelings of doubt to make the decision and let go. My relationship with the movement had been valuable and I knew that my exit would be impactful to me so careful consideration was required. I considered my experience over the years, talked to friends about the doubts and stayed tuned-in to how I was feeling throughout the process. I experienced a tension during this time, which I reacted to negatively. I wanted the decision to be made there and then. A tension such as this is actually a creative tension, which can be viewed positively if we are aware rather than getting lost in it. Our mind and body are both working together to create alignment with what is required for us.

If we understand our core values, we can use these to inform decisions. One of my core values is freedom so I often ask myself if activities or relationships create or reduce freedom. Freedom is not something that I can fully articulate. It is more of a feeling or knowing that I tune in to and respect. It is internal freedom in my mind rather than freedom on an external level. Freedom from resistance and suffering. Relationships in general, including those with teachers and religious movements, will increase freedom or reduce freedom. To sustainably be intrinsically connected to something and feel at peace, be it a religion, personal relationship or anything else, you must feel freedom within it and realize that it does not define who you truly are.

Spiritual Retreats

Spiritual retreats allow us to live in a place for a few days or weeks that offers an environment and routine which is different to our normal life and conducive to spiritual practice. This can be to practise meditation, listen to a spiritual teacher, learn yoga or partake in a variety of other activities. Given my experience and that of friends who have attended a range of different events and retreats across various countries and religions, I would like to introduce a list of considerations, which can be used to help inform decisions relating to selection and attendance:

- Firstly, ask yourself what you are looking to achieve by attending. If you have some goals in mind, then check to see how the retreat might help you to achieve them. You can usually access information on retreats through websites or by contacting the retreat organizers. Be aware of your motivations for attending.

- Consider the duration of the retreat. If this is your first retreat, you may choose to select a shorter duration before immersing yourself into something longer. The length of the retreat will influence the depth of your practice whilst you are there and also the opportunity that the teachers will have to influence you.

- Seek clarity on any religious content and ensure that you are comfortable before signing up. Find out if the organization and people hosting the retreat or the retreat location is connected to a religion. You can also ask if any religious rituals are practised, such as chanting, Puja or devotional practices. Some retreats hosted within a religious context may have an undercurrent to them which pulls some retreatants deeper into that religious movement. This may be engineered by the movement or happen quite naturally without a specific intention from those hosting the retreat.

- If an organization offering a retreat is religious, you can ask yourself whether you need openness to other religions as opposed to insisting that there is only one single path. Some movements offering retreats may be grounded in a specific religion whilst integrating others. I have attended yoga retreats in ashrams with a Hindu lineage. Those hosting the retreat were very devoted to their own teachers whilst inviting and integrating guest speakers from a range of other religions. Oneness and unity were actively promoted in these ashrams, which I experienced positively.

- Check out the retreat schedule, including timings for waking, eating, sleeping and anything else you will be doing there. Assess the intensity of the retreat. If it feels like it may be too much for you at this point in time, then consider a lighter option.

- Consider attending the retreat with a friend. If you are new to retreats, this can help with your confidence and provide support whilst you are there.

- If you already have a spiritual guide or teacher, you may speak to them about the retreat and consider their views.

- Many retreats are fully or partially held in silence and insist upon relinquishing mobile phones and other devices. Understand any expectations in these areas in advance.

- Perform an Internet search for reviews of the retreat, teacher or centre you are looking to attend. This will give you deeper insight into what you might expect should you attend, including the quality of the teachings. Many retreat centres are listed within tourist attraction review websites.

- Extract some background information on the teacher or facilitators if possible. Learn about their personal style and values to check if they are likely to be compatible with yours.

- I work on the assumption that most retreats will be of benefit to the attendees, be created with good intentions and facilitated ethically. There will always be some exceptions. I have been close to people who have suffered greatly, which they claim was triggered by unskilfulness on behalf of teachers at retreats. As well as considering the pointers in this chapter, you can set and review boundaries to help protect yourself whilst you are there in areas like diet, rituals, silence, communication and donations.

- The time leading up to a retreat and subsequent to the retreat are all part of the process and may be emotional. Consider whether you create space before and after by taking some additional time out to relax, prepare for the retreat and integrate your experience. Leaving a retreat can be a sensitive time. This is influenced by the difference in the retreat lifestyle and the lifestyle back home in your daily routine. You may choose to stay free of situations that are emotionally challenging or intoxicating on your return.

- Try not to create any new dramas in your life before departing for the retreat. If you have issues outside of the retreat, such as a bill you have to pay or an important call you need to make, these may interfere with the experience. It is ideal if you can leave your normal life behind peacefully. This will help you be better placed to concentrate and relax during your time there.

Spiritual retreats are a great place to meet new friends. Over the years, I have met some wonderful people on retreat from places all over the world and the friendships I created have been sustained and supportive. A good retreat environment and climate that is infused with Presence will enable deep bonds to be created quickly.

Studying Spiritual Teachings

A large proportion of my spiritual development has been supported through teachings made available through the Internet and books. Having a full-time job and parental responsibilities for the bulk of my adult life left little time for retreats and visits to teachers.

When you are accessing content create an environment where you can be Present and give the teachings your full attention. Select a quiet environment where you will have minimal distractions. Five minutes of accessing content with full concentration will provide far more benefit than accessing content for one hour with distractions. Avoid listening or watching content whilst doing another activity, especially if that activity requires your full awareness to be completed safely. This will be far more beneficial and safer for you than diluting the quality of both activities.

Many people find it helpful to stick with accessing content regularly from one or two teachers. The fewer teachers we access and the more that we access them, the deeper we will go with their teachings. Occasionally, there may be a particular theme we are studying which justifies accessing a range of content from a multitude of teachers allowing us to look at the theme through a number of lenses, which can prove useful and aid learning.

To benefit from spiritual teachings, a three-step cycle of hearing, reflecting and integrating needs to take place. Hearing teachings covers what enters our senses. Examples include reading a book, listening to a teacher in person or watching a video. Our mind then needs time and space to create linkages from what we have taken in through the senses to previous knowledge we have stored in our memory. This is called reflection. This process of reflection helps to embed the teachings. Once we can apply them spontaneously and consistently in our daily lives, the teachings become a part of us and are fully integrated.

Reflection can take place on a subconscious level. We hear a teaching that resonates with us and without any conscious effort, our minds work in the background to make links from the teachings to our existing knowledge. If our life is spacious, there will be more likelihood of this taking place. If our life is full or complex and we spend a lot of time thinking about other things, there will be little opportunity for this and less progress made. Reflection can also take place at a conscious level and be enabled through planning. For example, reading about a particular teaching in this book and then discussing it with a friend would be a form of conscious reflection. Other forms of conscious reflection include writing, journalling, mind mapping and sitting quietly, allowing the mind to contemplate a particular subject.

It is helpful to make time for reflection as part of our practice. It can be tempting to keep absorbing more and more teachings. Some people will read endless amounts of books or be continuously travelling around visiting teachers without taking the space to reflect and integrate what they have learned. Less is often more and it is sometimes beneficial to cut down on the amount we are absorbing to allow more time to reflect. Interestingly, reflection can also take place if we are listening to different teachings on the same subject. For example, we might hear a teaching from one teacher that resonates with us, hear something similar from another teacher and then link the two teachings together in our mind, deepening our understanding. Also, listening to teachings or reading books multiple times can support reflection, as each time we hear or read the content, we have the opportunity to create links to different items of our knowledge, dependent on what is relevant for us at the time. A quality spiritual book will have this effect. It is possible to read exactly the same book at different times and find some of the content to be completely fresh. The content is exactly the same. What is happening is that we are mentally creating fresh links from our own experience to the same teachings.

Time & Motivation to Study

For those who find it challenging to get motivated and create the time to study, then establishing a regular routine and studying little and often may help. I have heard many people tell me that they would love to study or meditate but do not have the time. To make time for practice, we can stop doing things that are unskilful. We can then use the time that is freed up for cultivating our practice. We let go of what is hindering us and replace it with what will help us. It is analogous to taking a step forward. To go on our chosen path, we have to remove our feet from behind us and place them in front of us.

We can start out by scheduling a small amount of time each week or month and then build from there. It can help to have a target for how much time we spend studying or have certain days and times when we plan to study. Another option is to study in a group or with friends on a regular basis. Many religious places including ashrams, monasteries and retreat centres make study a part of the daily routine for those in attendance.

For some, their character and situation may lead them to study excessively and part of their motivation for reading or accessing teachings via the Internet may be to avoid other ways of learning that are needed including through friendship, connecting with nature, meditation and the body. It is fine to immerse ourself in studying teachings intensively for a while, but at some point, we will need the time out to reflect and integrate those teachings into our life in order to realize the benefits.

Another option for studying is to join a local group that meets regularly. This provides some accountability and social contact that can help with motivation. An advantage of a group is that it can support reflection and learning through discussion. Effective groups create an environment for true listening that is accepting, non-judgemental and respects confidentiality. Effective groups also stick to the teachings and refrain from advising individuals on what they should or should not do. The advice in these contexts will often be ego-driven and work on a false premise that the person giving the advice knows what is best for others. As a general rule, unless the advice we are giving is very simple and obvious, then the best advice is not to advise. Attending groups is also a great way to create new friendships that are formed in a spiritual context.

If we find that we are resisting studying, surrendering and allowing a little more time with the content will often move us into a state of acceptance. If we are resisting studying on a sustained basis and cannot bring acceptance to it, then changes need to be made in terms of what, how, where or with whom we are studying. Also, it may be not the right time to study now or at any time in the future and that is absolutely fine. Study does not suit everybody and there are other options for practice to help us become more Present.

To summarize, spiritual teachings provide knowledge and pointers that can help us to become more Present. The knowledge and pointers are only helpful if they enable us to connect with the source that created them. Ultimately, the true measure of a person's spirituality or Presence has little to do with how much they can recall teachings and everything to do with how much they are connected with who they truly are.

POINTS FOR REFLECTION

- If suffering manifests naturally, we can learn from it and be grateful for our experience.

- There is no 'best' action or any real choice. There is simply a process, which takes everybody and everything into consideration.

- No single teacher or set of teachings can ultimately satisfy our entire spiritual needs.

- Our goal is to increase the amount of time we reside in Presence with the ultimate ideal of being Present continuously.

- For the majority of us, we will awaken gradually through practice.

- Every decision that we make in life, no matter how small, represents a T-junction and the direction taken influences the amount of peace or suffering we will experience in the future.

- We must never expect to be ultimately satisfied by a religion or teacher for two reasons. The first reason is that like us, the religion and teacher are all subject to change. The second reason is that all unenlightened humans are involved in the awakening process meaning that teachers may be unskilful at times.

- To sustainably be intrinsically connected to something and feel at peace, be it a religion, personal relationship or anything else, we must feel freedom from it and know that it does not define who we truly are.

- Spiritual retreats allow us to live in a place for a few days or weeks that offers an environment and routine which is different to our normal life and conducive to spiritual practice.

- The fewer teachers we access and the more that we access them, the deeper we will go with their teachings.

- It is helpful to make time for reflection as part of our practice.

- To make time for practice, we can stop doing things that are unskilful.

- For those who find it challenging to get motivated and create the time to study, then establishing a regular routine and studying little and often may help.

- To make time for practice, we can stop doing things that are unskilful.

- As a general rule, unless the advice we are giving is very simple and obvious, then the best advice is not to advise.

- The source of all spiritual teachings is infinite.

- Ultimately, the true measure of a person's spirituality or Presence has little to do with how much they can recall teachings and everything to do with how much they are connected with who they truly are.

OPTIONAL LEARNING ACTIVITIES

- Review the possibility of attending a spiritual retreat. Look around for options and work through the list of considerations provided earlier in the chapter.

- Create regular time for study and reflection on spiritual teachings.

- Explore the option of joining a local study group or meditation group.

- If you are religious or part of a religious movement take some time to review your relationship with that religion.

Chapter Twelve

Structuring Our Practice

The purpose of this final chapter is to help you structure your practice and select the most appropriate areas to work on. As you proceed, try and let go of thinking about results and allow them to manifest naturally. Thinking about being Present is not necessarily being Present. When we are Present, we do not need to think about it. Also, getting lost in some fantasy about achieving an enlightened state at some point in the future or becoming more "spiritually evolved" is a hindrance. Instead, we must return to the present moment and turn our attention to our own awareness in parallel with the activities that we are engaged in at the time. This is where we need to be and where we can only truly be.

As we select areas to work on and make changes to our mindset and conditions, we keep in mind that there will often be a difference between what we want and what we need. The ego demands what we want. Our true self invites what we need. Through our awareness, a tension is created between opposing wants and needs. For example, we may want to act out of an addiction, but what we need is to feel and transmute the underlying emotional pain. We may want to judge ourself, but what we need is acceptance. We may want to fill our lives with activities when what we need is more space.

You might recall from the introductory chapter that Presence can be cultivated through three approaches.

The first is through structured practice. This includes activities practised on a regular basis such as meditation, yoga or studying spiritual teachings. The second is through everyday activities like brushing your teeth, walking around, driving, using your phone or waiting in a queue. It may be easier to try integrating being Present into simpler activities to begin with, then to move on to more complex activities as your practice evolves. The third approach is changing our life conditions. For example, we may change how we work, the places we go, or let go of having so many assets. It helps to keep these three approaches in mind as we decide how we are going to cultivate Presence.

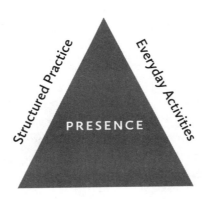

Life Conditions

Three Approaches To Cultivate Presence

An alternative way of viewing our endeavour to become more Present is through the lenses of inward and outward practice. Inward practice covers the inner work on ourself through care and cultivation of the mind and body. Meditation and yoga are examples of this. Outward practice is arranging our life conditions so that they are more conducive to being Present. An example of this is replacing some of our depleting activities with nourishing activities. Our conditions have a significant influence on our ability to stay Present, including what we do, how we do it, where, with whom, what we own and so on. If Presence was a packaged food, there would be a label on the side that says "Important: eating this product may result in significant changes to your life".

Inward practice and outward practice are intrinsically linked together and impact each other. Generally speaking, we find that when we are practising well inwardly, our life conditions generally fall into place to support us. Likewise, when we set up our outward life conditions, it becomes easier to practise inwardly.

Creating a Presence Inventory

To help us focus our practice, we can create an inventory of all the different activities that we are involved in. Driving, listening, eating, visiting the toilet, sitting in a meeting, making love, using our phone, walking, exercising and so on. Optionally, we can break this down further by adding context. For example, rather than just writing 'listening', we could write 'listening to Mary' or 'listening to work colleagues'. Our context significantly influences how Present we are. For example, we may be very Present whilst driving down the street where we live, but not so Present if we are driving on a highway. We may be Present when in the company of one group of people, but lost in thought or intoxicated when in the company of another group.

The length, level of detail or completeness of the inventory is unimportant. Its purpose is to get us thinking about how we are bringing Presence into our everyday activities. Put another way, how we are bringing being into the doing of our lives. Unless we are awakened, Presence is always context sensitive, which means it varies based upon what we are doing, how we are doing it, where we are doing it and with whom we are doing it. The reason for this is that the ego, which forces us out of Presence if we let it take over, only gets triggered based upon certain conditions.

Once we have our list of activities, we can then conduct a self-assessment giving ourself a score of one to five for each activity where one is consistently lost in thought and five is consistently Present. We can then use the list to decide where to focus our practice. Making a note of the date, when we conducted the assessment allows us to reassess later, compare the results and track improvements. We may notice a number of related activities where we are more Present or lost in thought, pointing to themes in our life that are helping or hindering us. It may be that we pick some easy areas to work with first, go for a major challenge or select a combination of the two. We may observe that by focusing our practice in one area, we naturally see improvements in others. Success breeds success with spiritual practice. It is fine to focus our practice on certain areas as long as it is against a backdrop of working towards a vision of being Present in all areas at all times.

Sometimes, it is impossible to decide upon an area of focus for our practice by thinking about it. Certain decisions are too complex to be solved with the thinking mind or it may not be the right time to make the decision. In these cases we ask ourself the question and then leave the rest to our subconscious mind and the changing conditions around us to guide us to the appropriate focus area when the time is right.

Even this process is an effective practice, as it requires faith and patience. It can be helpful to take a break from time to time and create space from consciously working on making progress. For some, creating this space is a practice in itself.

Striking the Right Balance

One extreme is to have no structure to our practice. We simply read what is covered in this book or other teachings and then assume we can implement the guidance spontaneously as and when required, becoming more Present without any planning or goal setting. The other extreme is to plan and structure our practice to the extent that we experience paralysis by analysis and become lost in the planning and thinking. Where we need to pitch ourself on the continuum of structure is a personal decision and will vary based upon the individual. For most, a middle way is best combining spontaneity and structure.

When prioritizing the areas we focus on, we can include some quick wins, which are things we know we can achieve soon with a little effort. This may be scheduling some mini meditations within the day or intensifying our awareness when we are around somebody that we find moderately difficult. Another example is mindfully eating our breakfast. Quick wins help us to appreciate the benefits of being Present, motivate us and build confidence, which can then be applied to bigger challenges. We may want to use our journal or calendar to write down what we plan to focus on for a particular week, month, quarter or year combining some short-term, medium-term and long-term goals.

Focus areas can be created with the support of friends. It can help to bounce our ideas off others that have known us for a period of time. These people can challenge us to ensure that any goals we are setting are reasonable. They can also hold us to account on progress. Spiritual practice may be uncomfortable at times and we may experience suffering. This is helpful, as our suffering will teach us. That said, our actions should never knowingly create suffering. This is analogous to effective exercise. We need to work to an intelligent edge where we push ourself out of our comfort zone, but not to the extent that it becomes painful.

Journalling & Writing

For some, keeping a journal can be beneficial. Journalling is a method of reflection and reflection is an essential part of learning. It helps us to identify recurring themes that we need to address, integrate what we study and celebrate our successes. We can select the frequency at which we would like to make entries in our journal. It may be that we make ad-hoc entries as and when the motivation arises or we have a more disciplined practice of journalling regularly. Another option is to target our journalling on key focus areas. For example, we can keep a meditation or communication journal. There is a range of journalling apps for those who enjoy using technology that run on computers and mobile devices.

Other forms of writing, in addition to journalling, can also be used to reflect. Writing this book has helped me to reflect upon the various teachings that I have read and listened to over the years and integrate them into my daily life. You don't have to create a book; keeping a journal, emailing a friend or writing a letter can all help. I have used mind maps in the past to capture and organize thoughts and feelings. Mind mapping suits those who have a visual preference and are structured in the way that they think and learn.

Practising with Others

Practising with others may help us to stay motivated, learn, reflect and meet our need for true friendship. Along the way, we will inevitably be faced with some big decisions or changes that come out of seeing clearly and acting wisely. We may need to change our job, let go of a relationship, face into a significant longstanding addiction or transform our social life to make it more ethical and skilful. Having people who can be with us in Presence as we consider and implement these changes helps us to gain perspective, clarity and provides much needed support. Here are some of the options that are available:

- Local groups meet regularly to meditate, discuss spiritual practice and explore teachings together.
- Religious movements and other organizations may offer environments and opportunities to create friendships conducive to practice.
- Spiritual teachers can play a part in supporting and guiding us. We may meet with them regularly to discuss progress and focus areas.
- Spiritual peers are friends who are at a similar level with their practice. We can meet regularly and provide support including encouragement and joint reflection.
- Becoming a spiritual teacher through giving talks or running groups, helps with our own personal development as well as creating a platform for others to practise. Teaching can ensure a deeper

understanding of the content we are working with and also provides an opportunity for us to learn from students.

- Specialist organizations can provide support with specific types of addictions. Engaging with them may mean regular contact with members of the support team there or inclusion in a regular group.
- A relationship with a therapist may be necessary to work on some specific areas that are hindering us which cannot be resolved alone, with friends or other groups.
- We may join an Internet-based online community of practitioners who are working towards the same goal and shared values.

These are just a few of the many ways that we can integrate others into our practice. Some find the thought of practising with people appealing and others have an aversion to it. Feelings of aversion and resistance are sometimes, but not always, calls to action to surrender to what we are resisting. The reality of our life is that we will need to be Present in solitude and Present with others so it makes sense to integrate both into our development. It is okay if our life sways towards a particular extreme for a time before regaining balance.

As mentioned earlier in the book, the people who we associate with will influence our practice. The association may be anything from having discussions with people to being in their physical proximity. Whilst it is not possible or recommended to cut ourself off from the world for long, it is sometimes helpful to manage our conditions so that we minimize the number of unconscious people we connect with. This may lead to friendships changing, being more selective about the places we frequent, and whom we might stand near or walk by in public places.

As our Presence increases, we will become better placed to retain our awareness when around others who are less conscious and we may even raise their level of consciousness in the process. It is a transition from skilful aversion to compassionate connection. That said, we do need challenges to make progress and these often take the form of interactions with people we find difficult. The key principle here is not to make life difficult by deliberately introducing challenges that test us. There will be just the right amount of these challenges heading our way naturally without us initiating them. If we seek out challenging people believing that they will help our practice they will hinder it. When difficult people are presented naturally and we are conscious around them, we cultivate Presence.

Progress & Measurement

In the interest of being open and honest, I would like to point out that I do not consider myself to be anywhere near fully awakened. I have not gone through a sudden transformational process, but have worked steadily with this practice over time and experienced significant improvements in the peace and happiness I experience. I have my faults and difficulties. I am often lost in thought and consider myself to be work in progress. There is really no need to judge or measure our own progress. However, given how most of us are conditioned, this is easier said than done. So if we do need to measure our progress, we should measure it over time and keep the measure simple. For example, we can ask ourself, "Do I feel more peaceful than I did a year ago?" or "Am I more accepting than I was six months ago?" We can also use a simple tool such as self-assessment, as described earlier.

We need to make allowances for our progress based on our conditions. For example, we may have experienced an unusually high level of turmoil in a significant area, such as a relationship or job, that may adversely impact our ability to stay Present. Sometimes these situations actually create more Presence. Friends, work colleagues and others that know us may offer feedback on our progress and positive changes without being prompted. If they are being honest and complimenting us with good intentions, this will signify that we are on track. Regular practice and steady progress is the aim, rather than perfection. If we practise and reap the benefits, we develop faith, which makes it easier to motivate ourself and build momentum.

It is quite natural for us to compare ourself to others. The comparison itself is harmless, but judging our conclusion as good or bad is harmful. For example, it is harmless to see somebody, make a comparison and conclude that they are taller than us. That is a fact that we have directly evidenced. It is harmful if we then go on to judge them or ourself as good or bad because of this. This type of judgement originates from our ego, which is based upon our identifications.

We are all far too unique and complex to make any helpful comparisons and judgements about what is good or bad. What appears to be a big difference to our ego is negligible on a universal scale. When we compare, we are comparing two people who are impermanent and in a state of flux. The accuracy of comparing how spiritual we are to others is limited, because we cannot see everything clearly. And at some point in the future, the basis of the comparison may change and become irrelevant anyway. Judgements and competitiveness originate from the ego and reinforce it whether we are comparing ourself favourably or unfavourably with others. The reason for this is that the comparison creates a separation between ourself and the person with whom we are making the comparison. Believing we are separate is delusional given that we are constantly changing and being influenced by the conditions around us, including each other. The truth is that we are all connected. We are all one.

Through reflecting on our comparisons, we can understand our attachments. We only unskilfully compare ourself to others when we are either attached to something that we have or are attached to the outcome of having something that we do not. If we do compare, we should reflect on the consequences, acknowledge the ego has made a comparison and then return to Presence, using one of the techniques in this book, such as anchoring our awareness to the breath. This may take some training if we regularly compare ourself to others.

Creating Time for Structured Practice

You can practise Presence at any time because Presence does not require time. Presence is timeless. However, if you engage in activities that enable structured practice, such as study, yoga or planned meditation, they do require time allocating to them. One of the most frequent challenges I encounter in others when I am teaching is their claim that they do not have enough time to do these things. There are three pointers that I provide:

1. **Prioritization** – We always have time available for structured practice. It is a question of prioritization. If we want to create time for activities that lead to Presence, we can stop unskilful activities that lead to being lost in thought. Put another way, we stop doing the things we should not be doing and start doing the things we should be doing. We let go of activities that deplete us and take up activities that nourish us. For most, this principle should be applied gradually over time. As a minimum, we can work on letting go of one unskilful activity and replacing it with something skilful. We might replace watching an unhelpful TV show with doing some yoga. We might move away from people who consistently complain and judge us and move towards those who are kind and accepting. We might let go of hanging out in intoxicating environments and start spending more time in nature. These are just a few examples and we have to

look at our own situations to determine what we should stop and start. We can use the Presence Inventory referenced earlier in this chapter to help us select the areas that need attention.

2. **Creativity** – If we cannot practise using one method, then we can try another. For example, to start with, many people find it difficult to integrate regular meditation into their busy daily schedules. We can find ways to creatively integrate mini meditations into our day. These could be before and after sleep, when we have parked our car, whilst standing in a queue or sitting on a train. If reading is difficult during study, then we can incorporate audiobooks or Internet audio/video content into our schedule. It is amazing how many options are available to us when we are creative.

3. **Planning** – We can use our calendar to plan our time on a weekly basis. Allocating times when we plan to do our various activities and then cultivating the discipline to do them adds some structure to our practice and creates positive habits.

Anchoring Our Practice

Until we are fully awakened, there is always the chance of slipping backward. We should be aiming forward and working towards becoming Present more of the time and ultimately all the time. The reality is that we may take two steps forward and one step back sometimes and that is part of the process. To keep us aiming forward, we need anchors. Anchors trigger us to cultivate Presence. Without anchors, we can easily drift and become lost like a boat out at sea with no direction. Before we know it, old habits return and we find ourself becoming lost in thought more of the time.

There are four types of anchor: structured, integrated, spontaneous and suffering.

Structured anchors are activities that we plan in advance with the intention that they are going to cultivate a state of Presence. Examples of structured anchors are meditation, spiritual study, yoga, reflection or taking a walk in nature. When we set the right intention, these activities allow us to become Present and set us up to bring more Presence into other activities.

The second type of anchor is an integrated anchor. These anchors do not require planning as they are integrated into regular activities. Examples may include bringing Presence into eating our breakfast, walking or listening.

We should identify one or two of these activities to start with and once Presence has become habitual, we can start work on others. Over time, our days will become saturated with these integrated anchors.

The third type of anchor is a spontaneous anchor. These are anchors that we do not plan or intentionally integrate into our activities. Examples include appreciation of beauty, suddenly becoming aware of a part of our body, or hearing a burst of delightful music. Over time and as our practice develops, these spontaneous anchors increase. We can experience Presence within and around everyone and everything once we know how. The Presence we are experiencing outside of us is shared and the same as the Presence we are experiencing within. No action is required to experience spontaneous anchors. They are the by-products and fruits of our practice.

If we do not enable our own anchors and are not receptive enough to experience spontaneous anchors, we can be sure that suffering, the fourth type of anchor, will point us in the direction we should be travelling. Suffering is the karmic reaction to being lost in thought. I am referring here primarily to psychological and emotional suffering. The intensity of the suffering matches the size of the jolt we need at the time to wake up and become Present.

Suffering can come along at any time. If we can, we should face our suffering fully, which means bringing full awareness and acceptance to the thoughts, feelings and bodily sensations that accompany it. By doing this, the form that is stored within our mind and body that triggered the suffering is eroded, which either reduces or removes the likelihood of it happening again. The opposite is to turn away from suffering, using tactics such as distraction or intoxication. This will always lead to more suffering and feed the ego. Every time we are Present, we weaken the ego. As we become more Present, we become skilled at noticing suffering and have the courage to face it rather than escape from it. We have to be capable and ready before doing this and in the meantime we should be accepting and kind to ourself.

Finally, I would like to point out that we can learn about various options for practice, analyse our situation and believe we are guiding ourself, but the truth is that Presence is guiding its own manifestation. Even without spiritual teachings, it will ultimately break through and guide us. Spiritual teachings and pointers are helpful. There is no doubt about that, which is why some of the great spiritual teachers in history, such as the Buddha and Jesus, are loved so much for their contributions. Teachings accelerate progress and create freedom from suffering. We can trust the universe to give us the teachings we need, when we need them.

POINTS FOR REFLECTION

- Presence is primarily about 'being'. Being who we truly are.

- Thinking about being Present is not necessarily being Present. When we are Present, we do not need to think about it.

- The ego demands what we want. Our true self invites what we need.

- Presence may be cultivated through structured practice, everyday activities and life conditions.

- It is fine to focus our practice on certain areas as long as it is against a backdrop of working towards a vision of being Present in all areas at all times.

- When prioritizing the areas we focus on, we can include some quick wins, which are things we can achieve soon with a few small changes.

- We may have drive within our practice, but we should never be driven.

- Practising with others helps us to stay motivated, learn, reflect and meet our need for true friendship.

- We need challenges to make progress and these often take the form of our interactions with people.

- Through Presence, we move away from people and situations that hinder us and towards people and situations that help.

- When we are in touch with who we really are, we will always know what to do, but may not always know why we must do it.

- We only unskilfully compare ourself to others when we are either attached to something that we have or are attached to the outcome of having something that we do not.

- We can practise Presence at any time because Presence does not require time.

- If we want to create time for activities that lead to Presence, we can stop unskilful activities that lead to being lost in thought.

- We may take two steps forward and one step back and that is part of the process.

OPTIONAL LEARNING ACTIVITIES

- Create a Presence Inventory of the different activities you are involved in and score the activities from one to five, where one is consistently lost in thought and five is consistently Present. Use the list to decide where to focus your practice and identify some quick wins.

- Create a journal, which can be used for reflection and learning. Decide if you would like to complete your journal on a regular basis and if so, set the frequency.

- Review some of the pointers earlier in this chapter to identify options for practising with other people.

- Review the amount of structured practice you are involved in on a regular basis. If you would like to create time for more, use prioritization, planning and creativity to create the time and motivation.

- Review anchors for your practice using the categories of structured, integrated and spontaneous anchors.

Afterword

It was a very special and creative time for me writing *Being Present* and I hope that your reading experience was the same. This book requires stillness to be read peacefully and beneficially. If you have read the book or even parts of it then congratulations as this means that the Presence has already started to awaken within you.

Once I had written the book I realized that it would help people be Present more of the time and also help to deepen the experience of Presence. This reflects the two dimensions of Presence, which are manifestation and depth. These are the primary formless or unconditioned objectives. The secondary form-based or conditioned benefits show up on the surface of life, which may include benefits in the areas of health, work, relationships and other external conditions.

Pause for a minute or two. Be aware of your experience. Connect with the breath, the body, look around your environment, be aware of what you can smell, hear, touch and taste. Be Present and experience the beauty. It is within and around you. If you make being Present your primary objective you will transcend to heights and experience depth that leads to absolute and timeless peace.

I wish you the very best on your journey.

Acknowledgements

I would like to thank friends that were involved in reviewing this book, *Being Present*. They enhanced the quality of the content far beyond what I could have achieved myself. They provided me with positivity, enthusiasm and faith. In particular, I would like to acknowledge Johanna Andersson, Jennie Hastings, Toby Henderson, John Rees, Shamus Shakil, Cassie Sobelton and Dennis Wareing. It also felt good to have the support and interest from my children.

Attendees at mindfulness programmes I was leading during the time of writing provided a constant reminder of how beneficial the teachings are. Their engagement, progress and appreciation motivated me to write. Our communication provided opportunities to gain deeper insights into the teachings.

Thank you to Eckhart Tolle[1] for his teachings in Presence and enabling me to make the connection. Sivananda yoga centres in Neyyar Dam, India[13] and Bahamas[14] gave me access to quality yoga teachings. Triratna Buddhist centres[15] in the UK and numerous helpful monks in Thailand helped me gain an appreciation of Buddhist Dharma. Having the opportunity to study, attend retreats and integrate with the various sanghas was essential for my spiritual development and the creation of this book.

Most of the book was written in the UK coastal town of Bournemouth. The natural beauty of the coastline, sea air, spaciousness and positive energy contributed to my general well-being and the creativity required during the months of writing.

Finally, thank you also to the publishing team at Findhorn Press who recognized this work and were prepared to invest into an emerging author. I appreciate and aspire to their essence to make a positive difference through spreading love, healing, peace and joy.

Notes

1. To learn more, see Eckhart's books *The Power of Now, A New Earth* or visit the Eckhart Tolle Now website. Details in bibliography.

2. Interpreted from definition provided in *A New Earth: Create a Better Life*.

3. Unskilfulness is harmful action (including thoughts, speech, physical acts or non-action).

4. Eckhart Tolle, *A New Earth: Create a Better Life* (London: Penguin, 2009), Kindle edition.

5. Control, when exerted unconsciously, is always based upon fear.

6. "The Five Mental Hindrances and Their Conquest", Access to Insight, accessed August 10, 2017, www.accesstoinsight.org/lib/authors /nyanaponika/wheel026.html#indiv.

7. It helps to differentiate need from greed. Greed is a desire for something you do not need.

8. Sharon Salzberg, *Loving-kindness: The Revolutionary Art of Happiness* (London: Shambhala Classics, 2002).

9. "Ask Deepak – What Is Ego", deepakchopra.com, accessed August 10, 2017, https://www.deepakchopra.com/video/article/801.

10. Eckhart Tolle. *The Power of Now: A Guide to Spiritual Enlightenment* (California: New World Library, 2004), Kindle edition.

11. "Eckhart Tolle Now", www.eckharttollenow.com, accessed September 7, 2017.

12. Chapter Ten explains why there is no such thing as a right job.

13. Sivananda Yoga Centre Neyyar Dam, http://sivananda.org.in/neyyardam.

14. Sivananda Yoga Centre Bahamas, http://www.sivanandabahamas.org.

15. The Buddhist Centre, http://thebuddhistcentre.com.

Bibliography

"Access to Insight – Readings in Theravāda Buddhism," http://www.accesstoinsight.org.

Ajahn Buddhadasa Bhikkhu. *Mindfulness with Breathing: A Manual for Serious Beginners*. Massachusetts: Wisdom Publications, 1988.

Burch, Vidyamala and Penman, Danny. *Mindfulness for Health: A practical guide to relieving pain, reducing stress and restoring wellbeing*. London: Piatkus, 2013.

"Five hindrances – Wikipedia," Wikipedia, accessed 27th July 2017, https://en.wikipedia.org/wiki/Five_hindrances.

Kamalashila. *Buddhist Meditation: Tranquility, Imagination and Insight*. Cambridge: Windhorse Publications, 2012.

Mason-John, Valerie and Groves, Paramabandhu. *Eight Step Recovery: Using the Buddha's Teachings to Overcome Addiction*. Cambridge: Windhorse Publications, 2012.

Ratnaguna. *The Art of Reflection (Buddhist Wisdom in Practice)*. Cambridge: Windhorse Publications, 2012.

Salzberg, Sharon. *Love Your Enemies: How to Break the Anger Habit & Be a Whole Lot Happier*. London: Hay House, 2014.

___*Loving-kindness: The Revolutionary Art of Happiness*. London: Shambhala Classics, 2002.

"Sivananda Yoga Vedanta Centres and Ashrams" http://www.sivananda.org.

Sri Swami Satchidananda. *Yoga Sutras of Patanjali*. Virginia: Integral Yoga Publications, 2012.

Subhuti, *Buddhism and Friendship*. Cambridge: Windhorse Publications, 2004.

Sutton, Nicholas. *Bhagavad-Gita*. Oxford: The Oxford Centre for Hindu Studies, 2014.

Tolle, Eckhart. *A New Earth: Create a Better Life*. London: Penguin, 2009, Kindle edition.

___*The Power of Now: A Guide to Spiritual Enlightenment*. California: New World Library, 2004, Kindle edition.

___"Eckhart Tolle Now," http://www.eckharttollenow.com.

Williams, Mark and Penman, Danny. *Mindfulness: A practical guide to finding peace in a frantic world*. London: Piatkus, 2011.

About the Author

DARREN COCKBURN has been practising meditation and mindfulness for over twenty years, studying with a range of teachers from different religions. Coaching and teaching groups in different contexts, he has supported hundreds of people in meditation, mindfulness and finding a connection to spirituality, with a focus on applying spiritual teachings in everyday life to cultivate a peaceful mind.

Darren also works as a business consultant supporting organizations with strategy formulation, interim leadership roles and transformation programmes. Outside of his work, he enjoys reading, walking in nature, spending time with friends and his two children. In addition, he is very passionate about yoga.

For more information and the opportunity to be trained or coached by Darren please visit his website: **www.darrencockburn.com**.

FINDHORN PRESS

Life-Changing Books

Learn more about us and our books at
www.findhornpress.com

For information on the Findhorn Foundation:
www.findhorn.org